YOU ARE NOT ALONE

Stories, Resources and Hope
from
Autism Moms

EDITED BY CATHERINE HUGHES

FORWARD BY DR. SHELLIE HIPSKY

YOU ARE NOT ALONE

STORIES, RESOURCES AND HOPE FROM AUTISM MOMS

Published by Grace and Hope Consulting, LLC
P.O. Box 104 - Dillsburg, PA 17019

Printed in the United States of America

ISBN: 9781701275157

Cover design by Jennifer Insignares, Motivated Mompreneurs
Cover photo by Braidan Abernethy
Additional editing by Cori Wamsley

DISCLAIMER AND/OR LEGAL NOTICES

Table of Contents

Acknowledgements

Catherine

I am grateful to my loved ones for their support of my calling which often takes up huge chunks of time from week to week. Through my work, I am richly blessed and can in turn bless others by sharing resources and stories of hope.

I am thankful to my son **Christian** for reminding me each day, no more how challenging it may be, that perseverance is the key to an abundant life.

My mother, affectionately known as **Mama Betty,** is my ear, my shoulder, my confidante, and my wings when I cannot fly.

My father, **John,** watches over everything I do from his utopia and smiles widely as I write. He knew Kissie was a writer all along.

In closing, thank you to this remarkable tribe—**Christina, Patti, Donna, Sarah, Jen, Holly, Lenore, Kelly, Chou, Hema,** and now **Shellie**—for believing in my leadership within this collaboration. Thank you for allowing me space in your hearts and to be a part of your journeys. Your friendship and your love make me whole.

Chou

I dedicate this chapter to my children. Thank you for teaching me so much about love, acceptance, life, and so much more. You fill my life with joy and purpose. You make me a better person. Thank you for being you.

Christina

To my husband **Jesse,** thank you for always being there through it all—the good, the bad, the ugly, and everything in between! I couldn't do this without you, and we are so blessed to have you in our lives. Thank you for everything you do for our family.

To **Selena and Braidan,** thank you for being the best sister and brother Ethan could ever have. The bond that you both have with him is pure love, and your dad and I could not be more proud. You are so lucky to have each other. I hope that you continue to stay close and always be there for one another.

To **Ethan**, my sweet Bubba, thank you for your kind heart, your silly personality, and the joy you bring to our family. You have a smile that can light up the darkest of days, and your laugh is truly contagious! I hope that you continue to bring joy into this world and show people that our differences are what make us all unique.

Thank you for teaching us what truly matters in life. Thank you for being YOU.

To all of the amazing coauthors, thank you for being on this journey with me. I am proud to be in your "tribe," and I'm grateful for each and every one of you.

Donna

Contributing to this book means the world to me, as do the ladies who join me in sharing our experiences. Endless gratitude and love goes to my family, especially my late sister **Cathy**, who left a legacy of enduring grace under extraordinary circumstances. Her example of finding inner strength set the stage for my autism years, and I strive every day to make her proud.

Hema

To **S.**, for being the amazing child who wakes up and fights the good fight to break the chains of autism.

To **A.**, for teaching us about unconditional love and patience and for being her brother's biggest advocate.

To **V.**, for bringing laughter back into our lives at a time when we needed it the most.

Holly

I want to thank God for choosing me to be **Sarah's** mother. Being a mother to her has transformed me into a kinder, more understanding, roll-with-the-punches type of person. It isn't easy, but through Him, all things are possible.

Obviously, a big shout out to my child, Sarah, who I wish I could be more like—unapologetically herself. I hope Mommy makes you proud with this book and even more, and I can't wait to see how you carry the torch of being a fellow advocate for others on the spectrum.

For my husband **Mike,** who makes me think that all my dreams are possible and who is my #1 fan, I appreciate that you are going along on the journey with us and have accepted and loved Sarah as your own.

And finally, a special thanks to the other authors of the book. Thank you for being "AUsome" moms and walking alongside me with this journey.

Jen

First, I have to say "thank you" to **my mom** for making me who I am today and for teaching me to be strong and fight for what is right. I miss her so much my heart hurts, but I know she is smiling down on me and helping to guide me to make the right decisions.

Second, to **Carly** and **Cassie**, thank you for making *me* a mom—the biggest honor I could ever possibly have. Carly, thank you for taking the back seat so many times when you should not have had to and for being the kindest and most compassionate teenager to ever walk the earth. Cassie, you have taught me more than I ever could have imagined: patience, fight, strength, and determination, just to name a few things. I know you will continue to bring joy to everyone whose lives you enter.

And finally, thank you to **Drew Engel** and his parents. Drew, you gave a terrible experience a happy ending and helped to remind me that there are more good people in this world than not. **Linda and Mark**, thank you for raising a young man who should be an example to all young people. You should be beyond proud of your son.

Kelly

I was asked to be part of this book and originally declined the offer. I wasn't sure what I had to contribute! The women on these pages are warriors, and I admired their voices in the autism community. Something kept tugging at me to do it, and three days before the deadline I decided to take part.

THIS tribe is the one I have been looking for. I want to thank each one of you for all the support with this book and the friendship that was built because of it. We have created a book of inspiration and resources. We have contributed our stories and fight every day toward fulfilling our commitments to our work, family, and our "AUmazing" children. I'm so proud to be part of this.

Shellie Hipsky, thank you for your contribution and commitment to this community.

My husband **Clint**, thank you for your unconditional love and support of our family. You are the definition of a husband and father.

Our daughters, **Ryley and Macy**, finding words to describe the beauty I see in your relationships with **Clayton** is impossible. Your support, listening, and love are appreciated more than you'll ever know.

My mom, **Mary Sue**, thank you for your support, helping when you didn't even realize you were by just being you.

To my friends and extended family who didn't walk away from us, you listened, even when I knew that you didn't even understand what I was talking about.

Clayton, you are my inspiration. You have made me a better person, you have already helped so many people and I know you have so much more to tell. I can't wait to see what you do with the many gifts God gave you. Thank you. I love you all.

Lenore

To **Paul,** you have cried with me, let me scream my lungs out, jumped for joy with me, and been there with me by my side.

To **Karl Joseph,** you have shown the world that we can survive autism with positive outcomes and that those with autism have a lot to contribute to society.

To **Paul Joseph,** you reminded me that I could handle challenges, when I did not think that I could. You made me laugh, you held me up, you had (and still have) faith in me.

To my **kitties**, animal therapy is special! You knew just when I needed extra love and came over to give it to me and to be by my side.

To the **Suvak Family** and the **Devlin Family**, THANK YOU for giving us the time away from the challenges of raising a son with autism. We so much appreciate all the times you took care of the kids for us so we could have some time to ourselves, as well as celebrating birthdays, holidays, and special occasions with us.

Patti

I'm forever thankful to God for my two biggest blessings, **Jordan** and **Nicole**. Jordan teaches me every day that learning and skill development never ends and there is joy to be found in the simplest of things. His smile lights up our world! Nicole can always make me laugh, and she challenges me to see things in different ways. She is an incredibly supportive sibling and my calm in the worst of autism storms.

I'm eternally grateful for my huge village of family and friends that have always included Jordan and who go out of their way to accommodate him and his needs. We are abundantly blessed!

Sarah

To **Glen**, my loving, supportive, hard-working, and amazing husband and father to our children—I wouldn't want to be on this journey with anyone else.

To **Colby and Tyler,** you've taught me so much in such a short amount of time—most importantly, you have taught me to be more patient, to look at life from a different angle, and to celebrate the little things. You both inspire me every day to be a better mom and person. Your unlimited energies, silly personalities, and bright smiles make you both one-of-a-kind. You will do amazing things in this life. I am so happy and proud to be your mommy.

Foreword

By Dr. Shellie Hipsky

"If anyone should have a kid with a disability, it should be me!"

I was in the fourth grade. It was in the evening after my class went on a field trip to the local school and workshop for people with challenges. My mom (who had been a special education teacher) listened to me proclaim this out loud emphatically and enthusiastically.

She went back to stirring a steaming pot of spaghetti while she thought for a moment. She glanced up and said, "Maybe one day, you will teach those kids."

At 12 years old, I went back to that same school and spent seven-hour days volunteering with children who were severely disabled and many who were on the autism spectrum.

One of the students, Becky, absolutely fascinated me.

Foreword

Close to my age, she would spin around in a corner making grunting sing-song noises. Becky was nonverbal, and the teacher I was helping at the time didn't engage Becky much at all. In fact, the teacher wasn't much of a role model for a future special education advocate. She used to say to me, "Don't teach this kind of student. It will drive you to drink!" I couldn't be swayed, though. I knew that I would someday give people with disabilities a voice.

The grumpy, jaded teacher just laughed in my face when I said I wanted to teach Becky how to talk. She allowed me to create a tiny makeshift classroom in a broom closet. I tried everything that I knew. Weeks went by, and both Becky and I were frustrated.

One day, a voice lesson that I was taking for my singing inspired an idea. When I met with Becky, I raised her hand in front of my mouth and said a word. Then, I placed my hand in front of her mouth. She stared at me, confused. I put her hand on my throat so she could feel the vocal movement and then repeated this with her own hand on her throat. We went back and forth until she had a lightbulb moment—the kind that teachers dream of their students having. A deep, rumbling, guttural "HELLO" came out of Becky's mouth! She was so excited! We both squealed and jumped up and down.

The most profoundly incredible moment for me, however, was when Becky's mother came to pick her up at the end of the day. Seeing tears flow down her mother's face when her daughter (who she was told was "never going to speak") said that one beautiful word, "hello," was everything.

Being a mother of any child is not easy. But when your child has challenges, days can be fraught with frustration, and the nights are often filled with endless worries.

I went on to become a special education teacher, ran a group home for autistic adults, and was an assistant principal at a K–12 school for students with emotional and behavioral needs who came from 40 different school districts. After I received my doctorate in educational leadership, I taught future special education teachers at the university level as a tenured professor at Robert Morris University for a decade. One of my thirteen books, *Differentiated Literacy and Language Arts Strategies for the Elementary Classroom* is a textbook that includes a collaboration with world-renowned expert in autism Temple Grandin, Ph.D.

My mother was right when she said I would go on to touch the lives of those impacted by the autism community! I absolutely adore this population and, since childhood, have strived towards giving people with disabilities a voice. It has been my privilege to also equip those who care for, educate or support them with the tools for success in addition to broadening their perspective— just like I did for Becky's teacher as a young girl with a dream.

I'm excited for you to find your tribe and to absorb helpful resources within the pages of this book! In addition to reading intimate testimonies from devoted mothers, you will also receive valuable pointers based on their lived experience, including:

- How you can move forward after receiving the diagnosis with a suggested "to-do" list of next steps

- How to decipher and digest the "the alphabet soup" of the autism world

- How to create personalized profiles and vision statements to express the strengths, needs, abilities, and preferences of individuals who need assistance in finding their voice and in cultivating their unique journey

- How to "find your tribe" which will help you identify local opportunities, build capacity and gain support through an entire network of parents and caregivers living in the trenches

- How to thrive, and not just survive, at an IEP meeting

Today, I'm the CEO of the motivational media company Inspiring Lives International, the president of The Global Sisterhood charity, author of the international best-selling trilogy *Common Threads,* and editor-in-chief of *Inspiring Lives Magazine.* Through print and social media I have embraced powerful connections. I am proud to highlight incredible women from all backgrounds but have found "common threads" with many women I have interviewed who have experienced disability themselves or raised someone with their own diagnosis and challenges—all of whom have conquered all kinds of obstacles and discovered their own definition of success. I humbly consider the world to be my classroom, and it is a blessing. My life truly came full circle.

I hold a special space in my heart for all mothers, and especially those who raise children with special needs. As a mom now myself (with one of my children considered to be non-neurotypical), I was so moved by Catherine Hughes' remarkable story about how she learned of her son's diagnosis, which she vulnerably shares in this book. I first heard it during our *EmpowerU* masterclass, and I was compelled to support her, as well as my friend Kelly Cain, who is a director at the Autism Caring Center and also a mother. Catherine and Kelly introduced me to this cohort of extraordinary accomplished mothers—Chou, Christina, Donna, Hema, Holly, Jennifer, Lenore, Patti, and Sarah—who also shared their stories and are changing this world. I was motivated to support them and push this compilation into the sometimes shaking hands of mothers across the globe!

I am confident that you will find yourself nodding in agreement as you affirm with your new tribe the struggles and triumphs of being a truly "ausome" mom, perhaps looking in the mirror with only your tear-stained face looking back at you while you say aloud with confidence, "I am not alone. Not anymore."

Photographer: Kevin Sheffield

Dr. Shellie Hipsky dedicates her life to empowering women globally to achieve their dreams. She began Inspiring Lives Magazine—*now nationally available—to focus on positive stories and spotlight people, especially women, who overcome the odds, help others, and positively impact the world. The crown jewels of her* 12 *published books, her international bestseller* Common Threads *trilogy, is based on* 100 *interviews from her Empowering Women Radio show. Her thirteenth book is due to be released in May 2020.*

Dr. Shellie also created the nonprofit 501 (c)(3) The Global Sisterhood and remains at the helm as president, guiding the charity to support women and girls toward achieving their dreams and goals. As an entrepreneur, she has been lauded with Entrepreneur of the Year in Inspiration and Empowerment, the Women of Achievement Award, Best Woman in Business, and VIP Woman of the Year, among other awards. She has graced over 20 magazine covers.

A former tenured professor of Ph.D. students at a private university, she stepped out of traditional academia and made the world her classroom by teaching business and nonprofit leaders with her EmpowerU Master Class and from the stage in front of thousands from the United Way Powerful Connections for Women to the University of Oxford in England. Dr. Shellie truly believes that "inspiration is just a story away!"

ATA - All. Those. Acronyms.

By Sarah Parks

The world of ASD (Autism Spectrum Disorders—Look! There's another one!) is full of acronyms—enough letters to make pots full of alphabet soup! Here are just a few of those acronyms and what they stand for to help guide you on your journey along the spectrum.

AAC - Assistive Augmentative Communication

ABA - Applied Behavior Analysis

ABLLS - Assessment of Basic Language and Learning Skills

ADA - Americans with Disabilities Act

ADD - Attention Deficit Disorder

ADHD - Attention Deficit Hyperactivity Disorder

ADOS - Autism Diagnostic Observation Scale

AIT - Auditory Integration Training

AS - Asperger's Syndrome

ASD - Autism Spectrum Disorder

ASL - American Sign Language

BCABA - Board Certified Associate Behavior Analyst

BCBA - Board Certified Behavior Analyst

BIP - Behavioral Intervention Plan

BT - Behavior Technician

CARS - Childhood Autism Rating Scale

CDD - Childhood Disintegrative Disorder

CF - Casein-Free

DAS - Developmental Apraxia of Speech

DD - Developmental Delay (sometimes referred to as "Global Developmental Delay")

DIR (Floor time) - Developmental, Individual-differences, Relationship-based

DS - Disability Services

DSS - Department of Social Services

DSM-5 - Diagnostic and Statistical Manual of Mental Disorders

DTT - Discrete Trial Training

EI - Early Intervention

ER - Evaluation Report

ESY - Extended School Year

FAPE - Free and Appropriate Public Education

FBA - Functional Behavior Assessment

FERPA - Family Educational Rights and Privacy Act

GARS - Gilliam Autism Rating Scale

GE - General Education

GF - Gluten-Free

HFA - High-Functioning Autism

IA - Instructional Aide/Assistant

ID - Intellectual Disability (sometimes referred to as "IDD")

IDEA - Individuals with Disabilities Education Act

IED - Intermittent Explosive Disorder

IEP - Individualized Education Plan

IFSP - Individualized Family Service Plan

ITP - Individual Transition Plan

LCSW - Licensed Clinical Social Worker

LEA - Local Education Agency

LFA - Low-Functioning Autism

LRE - Least Restrictive Environment

LSW - Licensed Social Worker

MA - Medical Assistance (Medicaid)

MAWD - Medical Assistance for Workers with Disabilities

M-CHAT - Modified Checklist for Autism in Toddlers

MDR - Manifestation Determination Review

MSDD - Multisystem Developmental Disorder

MT - Mobile Therapy/Therapist

ND - Neurodiverse

NIH - National Institutes of Health

NIMH – National Institute of Mental Health

NOS - Not Otherwise Specified

NT - Neurotypical

OCD - Obsessive Compulsive Disorder

OCR - Office of Civil Rights

OHI - Other Health Impairment

OVR - Office of Vocational Rehabilitation

ODD - Oppositional Defiant Disorder

OT - Occupational Therapy/Therapist

PALS - Peer-Assisted Learning System

Sarah Parks

PANDAS - Pediatric Autoimmune Disorders Associated with Strep

PBIS - Positive Behavioral Intervention and Supports

PCA - Personal Care Aide/Assistant/Attendant

PDD - Pervasive Developmental Disorder

PDD-NOS - Pervasive Developmental Disorder, Not Otherwise Specified

PECS - Picture Exchange Communication System

PLEP or PLP - Present Level of Educational Performance

PRT - Pivotal Response Training

PT - Physical Therapy/Therapist

RBT - Registered Behavior Technician

RDI - Relationship Development Intervention

RS - Rett Syndrome

RTI - Response to Intervention

SAS - Supplementary Aids and Services

SCD - Social Communication Disorder

SCD (*why yes, there are two!*) - Specific Carbohydrate Diet

SED - Serious Emotional Disturbance

SF - Soy-Free

SI - Sensory Integration

SIB - Self-Injurious Behavior

SID - Sensory Integration Disorder/Dysfunction

SLD - Specific Learning Disability

SLP - Speech-Language Pathology/Pathologist

SSI - Supplemental Security Income

SSDI - Social Security Disability Income

SSRI - Selective Serotonin Reuptake Inhibitor

TEACCH - Treatment and Education of Autistic and Related Communication Handicapped Children

TP - Treatment Plan

TS - Tourette Syndrome

TSS - Therapeutic Support Staff

VB - Verbal Behavior (sometimes known as "Applied Verbal Behavior")

VB-MAPP - Verbal Behavior Milestones Assessment and Placement Program

Breaking the Silence

Christina Abernethy

"Once you choose hope, anything is possible."

~ Christopher Reeve

"Nonverbal." I remember hearing that word and thinking, "What does that even mean? What do you mean my son is *nonverbal*?"

A thousand things ran through my head . . .

Will he ever talk?

Will he be able to say "Mom" and "Dad"?

Will he say "I love you"?

A hundred different emotions filling my soul, and the strongest of them all was fear.

What if he doesn't ever speak verbally?

What if we never hear his voice?

1

Breaking the Silence

What if he can't communicate?

What does that look like for him? Or for our family?

I was so scared and worried about the future. The thought of the unknown started to consume me. It would take my breath away the longer I thought about it. I knew I couldn't stay in that mindset and that I needed to act quickly.

So I turned all of my emotions into purpose. I knew we had to get our son help to speak. Even if he can't say words verbally, he needed the tools to help him communicate!

We started with sign language and also enrolled him in speech therapy. I knew how beneficial both could be for our son, so we started right away. We used sign language videos to help us learn how to sign, and he soon loved it! We would watch the videos and learn new signs together as a family. It was amazing!

As he grew older and verbal speech was still not present, his speech therapist introduced picture cards. He was able to point to pictures and let us know when he was hungry or if he wanted a drink. From there, they recommended a speech device, or as we call it a "talker." Alongside speech therapy, we were also encouraging him to communicate with us by pressing buttons on his device. In time, Ethan (our "Bubba") was able to say "eat," "drink," "play," "dinosaurs," and more with his talker!

As time went on, Ethan would press a button on his "talker" and then try to repeat it! For example, he would hear "apple" on his speech device and say "ah!"

It was so awesome to watch him in action, but most importantly, to finally hear his little voice.

Whether we were signing or using his device, we never stopped verbally repeating the words, too. It's always been very important to us to be consistent and keep in mind that the big goal is for him to communicate fluently with verbal speech.

Ethan's device and signs continued to encourage his speech development. However, it was still a struggle to truly understand and know what he wanted or needed, when he wanted or needed it.

It is so hard as a parent to not know how to help your child. Do you know what that feels like?

If you're nodding your head right now, please know that you are NOT alone!

Are they in pain?

3

Breaking the Silence

Are they sick?

Are they scared?

Are they nervous?

It's a guessing game, and you're never really sure if you're right.

But no matter what, we refused to give up hope. We would never stop trying new things that we thought might help our son communicate.

Years of trial and error, ups and downs, lots of tears, and then one day . . . there it was.

"Mom."

Wait, what?!

Did he just say that? Did my little boy just say "Mom"? Did that word just come from our Bubba?

YES, IT DID! And then, he said it again!

"Mmmmmmmoooooooooooooooooooooooom m!"

The sweetest sound I've ever heard in my entire life happened that day in our living room. It was a day I wasn't sure would ever come but fully believed that it would! I will never forget the excitement in his face. I will never forget the happy tears and our entire family clapping for him. His brother and sister both hugged him tightly. Celebrating the moment together made my heart explode! It was a day our family will cherish forever.

Just a few weeks later, he said "Dad"! I've never seen my husband's face light up with so much joy.

That's when I knew that he still had so much more inside of him! I can see in his eyes how badly he wants to communicate with us. I started looking for something more, something we haven't tried that might be *THE* key. That one class or that one therapeutic approach that will help him soar!

I am very active in the autism community, and I enjoy being a part of groups and helping other families. I also enjoy learning from other parents and getting ideas of new things to try or therapies to research. I had heard about music therapy, but I didn't understand exactly what it was.

Was it like a music class? Does it teach children with different abilities how to play instruments? Does your child listen to different types of music that could be therapeutic to them? I had no idea, but I definitely wanted to learn more to see if it was something we could try with Ethan.

Breaking the Silence

After doing some research, connecting with friends, and calling different programs, we found one that we thought would be perfect for our Bubba, and we enrolled him in classes! His music therapy sessions are 30 minutes long, and they incorporate music as a means of helping children talk, learn, play, and engage in social situations. They also learn colors, their ABCs, numbers, and shapes all while playing music and singing songs that the child loves! They even do a little dance sometimes, which Bubba just loves.

Every session is different and is adapted for each child. They base the sessions around your child's needs or wants on that particular day, which is amazing.

Since day one, they have sung a "hello" song at the beginning of the session. The music therapist will play her guitar and sing, "hello hello hello," and then our son is supposed to answer back "How are you?" Then together they will sing, "It's time for music."

Bubba would sit and smile or he would dance along to the guitar while his therapist sang. After a couple months of sessions, one day when his therapist started singing and playing her guitar . . .

"Hello hello hello," she sang.

From Ethan's lips, we heard: "How are you?"

This is the part where I practically fell off my chair and started ugly crying. I went running over to him to give him the biggest, proudest mom hug and kiss ever! I even considered hugging the music therapist because I was just so happy and excited for him.

Three words! THREE words! In. A. Row.

I still get goosebumps thinking about it. This boy never ceases to amaze me! He works so hard day in and day out just to be able to do things that come so easily to others, but he NEVER gives up.

Autism has taught me to never take life for granted. It has taught me to treasure every milestone and goal accomplished, no matter how big or small. It has taught me strength and patience that I never knew I had. It has taught me to never give up hope, and never lose sight of what's truly important in life. It has shown me that autism does NOT define him. Autism is just a part of our sweet, funny, silly little boy who loves dinosaurs and trains!

Our journey is far from over, and there is still hard work to be done. We will continue to guide him and support him every single day no matter what it takes! I know with every ounce of my being that our sweet Bubba will be able to have conversations with us some day. He's already come so far, and has worked tirelessly to get where he is today. We have spent years trying to help him find and use his voice.

Every single therapy session, every appointment, and every meeting is truly worth it, and I would do it ALL over again.

Always remember that you are not alone, and never give up!

It's never, ever too late to ... *break the silence.*

Christina Abernethy

Photographer:
Jackie Carlantonio

Christina is a dedicated wife, mother of three, and passionate advocate for people impacted by disabilities. She has coordinated events to fund research, support, and service dogs for families. She has served on local committees, coached an adaptive cheerleading team, and won awards for successful fundraising endeavors, including those for "Team Bubba," honoring her son with autism.

She serves as a Family Support and Community Engagement Specialist at Achieving True Self. She is the founder of Love Hope and Autism and is proud to be the coordinator for Changing Spaces Pennsylvania, a movement to build accessible restrooms with powered height-adjustable adult-sized changing tables across communities to promote inclusion. She is working with legislators to pass a bill in

Breaking the Silence

Pennsylvania that would require such facilities in hospitals, airports, museums, rest stops, sports arenas, and more. Christina is committed to spreading a message of heightened awareness and acceptance of differences, ultimately inspiring hope. For her efforts, she won the ACHIEVA Award of Excellence for Family Supports in 2018.

Cassie's Voice

Jennifer Bruno

"Anyone can give up. It's the easiest thing in the world to do. But to hold it together when everyone would understand if you fell apart ... that's true strength."

~ Chris Bradford

For any parent or caregiver of a child with autism reading this, you know how much of a mental and emotional struggle it is to take your child to an event or activity that is not a part of your normal routine. You imagine every possible scenario in your head, knowing very well that you will be thrown some sort of curve ball that you didn't see coming.

You second, triple, and quadruple guess yourself and talk yourself out of going at least 10 times before you finally put on your big girl pants and venture out into this sometimes cruel world.

What was intended to be just a quick trip to a high school swim meet to support our neighbor at her senior night, turned into one of my worst nightmares.

I knew attending would be hard for Cassie. She is visually impaired AND she has autism, so I knew it was risky to take her to a pool. She would smell the chlorine and think she could swim. It would be full of echoes and very humid; all of the ingredients for a perfect storm. It was all of those things, just like I knew it would be. But my older daughter insisted that going was the right thing to do. She said that our neighbor would be so happy that we were all there for her. Cassie has very few "friends," but the kids in our neighborhood are all so accepting of her and she loves all of them.

So we did the thing I knew we shouldn't do.

Now let me clarify: I had never been to a swim meet before this night. I didn't know if there was swim meet "etiquette," but I became concerned with Cassie's typical outbursts during the diving portion of the meet. I even turned to my neighbor sitting next to me and said, "We are going to get kicked out of here because Cassie is going to cause someone to slip off the board and hit their head."

I tried giving Cassie my phone to listen to music or one of her favorite stories to keep her occupied, but my older daughter said it was too loud. I tried giving her earbuds, but she wouldn't leave them in her ears.

I also want to clarify that she was NOT yelling non-stop. She was excited and maybe a little anxious because this event was out of the norm for us. She would yell out every so often. Of course, many athletes and spectators stared (which I am used to when we go anywhere), but at this point in our journey, I am able to ignore almost all of it.

Immediately after the senior recognition portion of the meet, we were approached by one of the coaches and the site administrator. I was told that the coach from the opposing team was concerned that Cassie's outbursts may cause one of his athletes to false start but that we were welcome to stand in the hallway and watch from the window.

I honestly don't remember if I responded. In my 15 years of being a parent, 13 years of which were spent raising a child with special needs, I have never felt more isolated, humiliated, and embarrassed as I did at that moment. I grabbed Cassie's cane and we left the pool area.

We were followed by four of the other neighborhood students, my older daughter Carly, our adult neighbors and a few other adults who were standing near the door. One of these adults happened to be a former employee of our district, and she said "We all love Cassie. Everyone who works with Cassie loves her. I can't even believe this is happening."

I don't know for sure that any of the neighborhood kids fully comprehended what transpired, but what I witnessed over the next hour was one of the most special moments I can recall in my adult life.

Students were in tears because Cassie was asked to leave. They were saddened by the fact that Cassie was singled out and treated differently because of her challenges. These youth ranged in age from 11–15, an age group where kids are more apt to bully than choose compassion.

They were hurt.

They were angry.

This happened in OUR school district—the district where Cassie should be considered "one of their own," the district where I send both of

14

my daughters each day with the assumption that the administration will not only educate my children, but advocate for them and look out for their well-being.

I choose to believe that everything happens (to me, anyway) for a reason. I made the decision to attend this swim meet. The fact that we were asked to leave the pool area after the senior recognition portion was God's way of nudging me to tell my story and educate communities so something like this might never happen to another family. Right, wrong, or indifferent, I reached out to some folks I know who broadcast for one of the local news stations in Pittsburgh. I went live on Facebook and told my story from start to finish.

My "job" as Cassie's mom is to make sure this world is as accepting of a place as possible for her, until I can no longer serve that role in her life. I take that responsibility more seriously than any other role I have ever played. I will always be her voice in a place where she does not have one. I will defend my actions to include her in any and all activities that she deserves to be part of fully and unquestionably. If this means that I have to make someone "feel bad" because "they have never dealt with autism before," then that's what I will do, even though my intention is just to educate.

If you are reading this book and you don't have a loved one on the autism spectrum, let me try to express this in a way you will understand and ask some questions. Do you have a "typical" child? Or even a pet? Think back to when your child was an infant, and the only way to communicate was through crying. As a new parent, you had no idea why your baby was crying, right? If you have a pet, when your pet is not acting as they normally do, they have no way to tell you what is wrong, correct?

Welcome to life every day for those of us with a child on the spectrum who struggles with effective communication. As parents, we do the best we can with what we know and what we are given. We make gut decisions and we hope and pray that they are the right ones for our kids.

But for all the rough waters we must navigate, there are many blessings. Allow me to share some more about my beautiful Cassie.

She loves to sing! She has performed at school talent shows, recitals, fundraisers, and sporting events and has even been known to belt out songs in the middle of a store, entertaining all around her! Some favorites include *All of Me, The Climb, Hey There Delilah, Bad Romance, Like a Virgin, In Case You Didn't Know,* and many others crossing all genres of music. I am always amazed with the different songs she chooses.

I love to guess what song Cassie is singing, because she usually doesn't start from the beginning. Cassie's dad ran the Pittsburgh Marathon blindfolded in 2013 and 2014 to raise money for different charities. In 2016, he pushed her in a stroller in the Pittsburgh Marathon while he ran. In 2017, Cassie ran the Pittsburgh Children's Marathon for one mile tethered to her father . . . and made ESPN's *Top 10 Moments in Sports* that same week! WTAE Channel 4 in Pittsburgh has produced several stories about Cassie, initially covering the marathon stories and then showcasing her love of singing.

My hope and prayer is that she continues to be a bright light in this world—which can sometimes be very dark—and a source of inspiration for those who may be facing their own challenges.

My intention for anyone reading my chapter is to encourage you not to limit your lifestyle because of challenges, either yours or of your loved ones'. Yes, you may encounter obstacles and bumps in the road, but that is the reason to grow and change from each experience, as well as perhaps change others.

Cassie's Voice

If you are a parent of a child with a diagnosis, take the risk and do something out of the ordinary. And I encourage every parent of every child—diagnosis or none—to always do the right thing. Teach your child to be kind to others. Preach that the world revolves around differences. Teach your child that everyone is different, and nobody is perfect.

Each child has a special place on this Earth, and for the world to be in harmony, everyone needs to understand that.

Jennifer is a mom of two girls, Carly and Cassie. She helped create Team Cassie, part of help support local special

Photographer: Carly Bruno

needs families and children by providing grants for bicycles or activities. The first grant was awarded to the Western PA School for Blind Children, and with continued fundraising efforts, the family hopes to provide more grant opportunities to others in need. Jennifer continues to be an advocate for her daughter and is working with her local school district to provide additional education to its staff and student populations. She also works full time as a divisional director for a healthcare company. In her spare time (HA!), she enjoys reading and refinishing old furniture.

I Thought You'd Never Ask

Kelly Cain

"The first step to receiving an answer is being brave enough to ask a question."

~Anonymous

It was so hot on that August day, now forever known as "diagnosis day."

We were stuck in construction traffic, the air-conditioning in the car was broken, and I was anxious. We were on our way to be seen at the Child Development Unit in Pittsburgh after waiting for over six months. The heat and the traffic only added to my—*our*—anxiety.

Clayton didn't seem to mind being stuck in traffic, strapped in tight to his car seat. He never complained at all. He often kept us guessing.

We had previously mentioned to the pediatrician our concerns. His response was, "We don't worry until they are three years old."

At a well-child checkup in March that year, we finally obtained the referral for an expert opinion on Clayton's behaviors, his lack of speech, and lack of development.

So many memories come to mind when I think about what Clayton was doing at that age. He wouldn't sit still for anything. He wouldn't look me—or anyone else—in the eye. I remember trying everything to please him: different bath times and bedtimes, new formula, switching his clothes, reading more books (or sometimes reading less), upgrading him to a big boy bed in which I would sleep with him or sometimes let him cry it out.

Nothing worked, it seemed, especially not "time out."

He didn't talk. Or maybe he didn't want to. Subdued behaviors were even more concerning. The only time he would look at me was in the bathtub. He would stare right at me with those big blue eyes, and I would cry and wonder, "What is going on with this sweet boy?"

Clayton is our youngest child, loved and doted on by older sisters. He never needed to ask for much, and always seemed like he just wanted to keep up with them. I knew though that he was struggling, and I had to help him.

I remember Christmas morning when he was 18 months old: all the lights, all the presents, and the excitement of Christmas. He stepped over all the presents and sat down to play with his toys. It was just like any other day.

Today, I thought, was going to answer all of the questions and concerns of the last two years.

We finally made it through traffic, filled out a mountain of paperwork and waited some more. I was fearful that if I didn't answer something correctly or leave out any details about his behaviors or delays that they would say, "He is just a boy," like many others had before them.

Two young doctors came in and began to go over our paperwork, verify our answers, and review our concerns. Clayton was lying on the floor, playing with trains, and just like that Christmas morning, he didn't seem to notice when they walked in. The doctors started to whisper and then excused themselves. Later, they came back.

One doctor asked us, "Do you mind if I touch him?" We shook our heads. He started on the back of his legs, pushing with his hands, and even patted his head.

Clayton never flinched. They tried again and again to engage him.

"Is he always like this?" the doctor asked.

"Yes," I confirmed. "I have a list of concerns and examples."

"Mrs. Cain, was your pregnancy normal?"

"Yes. My first pregnancy was not. I was toxemic at three months, and I failed every blood test."

"Really?" he asked.

"Yes. This pregnancy was easy," I told him.

Then ...

"Based on our observations and your concerns expressed, we are sure of our diagnosis of autism."

Silence.

We didn't look at each other. I didn't know—and I knew my husband didn't know—what autism was. My husband asked, "Will he have this the rest of his life?"

"Yes," one of the doctors said, "and he will probably never speak. This diagnosis will label him as 'disabled.' You will need a provider to coordinate services. He will also need state insurance because private insurance will not cover his therapies."

Disabled? Service Provider? Therapy?

I asked, "Can you tell me how to help him?"

"Mrs. Cain, you cannot help your son. He needs more than you. I am very sorry. The receptionist will give you all the information you need. Good luck."

Good luck?!

None of my questions were answered. Is autism why he only eats in the bathtub? Is autism why he doesn't look at me? We left with a huge packet, full of words I didn't want to learn or understand.

Autism?

In the car, my legs melted into the seat, and I started to cry—hard. Not understanding a thing, none of our questions answered, I felt that instead of getting clarity, things seemed even worse. I felt trapped.

We had no choice but to dive in. I had to learn the language of autism, specialists in my house, sensory issues, behavior therapy, sign language, special schools, and private schools. We were fighting for him to become verbal. We were learning how to tiptoe through this world, observe him, and learn his triggers. We were fighting to be a normal family of five. We were trying to explain something I barely understood to family, friends, and his sisters.

I started blaming myself and went over my pregnancy in my head. What did I do wrong? What did I do differently? What baby food did I feed him? What is in our water? What happened in three short years?

My husband said to me, "It doesn't really matter now. What matters is how we move forward." He was right.

We moved forward one step at a time, sometimes falling but always getting back up while questioning every decision. We were (still are) constantly learning, not always from doctors or therapists. We learn from Clayton himself through the meltdowns in restaurants, meltdowns in school, all of the stares, all of the screams, and all of the sleepless nights.

One frustrating day, Clayton's very first behavior specialist said to me, "What you are seeing is part of the diagnosis. He can't change. You will have to adjust. This is the new normal." That stuck with me.

Every time I wanted to give up, I thought, "No, I can keep adjusting until he succeeds, crosses a hurdle, or overcomes that barrier. She was right: he hasn't changed. Today, he manages more effectively, and his environment is adjusted, but not so much that he is not challenged to learn in school and be part of the community he lives in.

So often, we have found ourselves splitting up as a family to go to events and to church. We didn't have a family outing for years. Sometimes, we still don't. The five of us have done more apart than together. The family strain is real and frustrating.

Clayton eventually started talking, at age seven to be exact. And finally at age 11, he made his first friendship. Speech and language therapy was our longest approach: he finished at age 13. We proved those first doctors wrong—he did speak, and I knew there was so much more he was able to do. We fought our way through school, for him to stay within typical classes, and even helped his teachers learn about autism along the way.

He is currently a sophomore in a mainstream school. Our son, who was never supposed to talk, stood up one day in his government class and gave an unplanned recap on current events. His teacher was so impressed, and he let all of Clayton's other teachers know. The administration heard about this accomplishment, and he was asked to give his story—yes, his personal account of his journey with autism—to professionals in the district.

I was apprehensive. The talking points were questions I had never asked him. "What is it like to have autism? What is it like to have sensory issues?" Sitting at the kitchen table, I wasn't sure if he would be able to answer those questions.

To my surprise, he looked right at me and explained in detail.

Just like that day in August, I was stuck in my seat at the kitchen table. Clayton talked for 15 minutes about autism, his sensory issues, overcoming barriers, and what he thinks needs to change.

Stunned, I said, "I can't believe you said all of that! I am so proud of you. I can't believe that's all in your head."

Clayton said to me, "I've just been waiting for someone to ask me."

He did accept the invitation to speak. That day, in front of 17 paraprofessionals, a young man who was told he would never gain verbal speech gave his story and shared his journey with autism.

Our son has overcome so much. I cannot wait to see and hear what else he does. He can now tell his own story. When he does, I will probably be stuck in my chair, and I will be the one speechless.

Don't ever give up. Don't ever quit asking the hard questions or asking for accommodations. Find the right tribe, the right doctor, and the right people for your child. If we had gone home that day and buried our heads in the sand, he wouldn't have had a chance.

YOU can do this.

YOU can raise this child.

YOU do have it in you.

Photographer: Macy Cain

Kelly Cain is from Pittsburgh, PA, and is a director at the Autism Caring Center, which was founded in 2017. Advocacy, professional training, support groups and family activities are provided free of charge. She is also a founding board member of PALS (Providing Assistance, Love and Support) a free recreational program approaching its ninth year of support for special needs families. In August 2019, she received a District 1 Difference Maker Award from Councilmen Sam Demarco and Tom Baker for her outstanding community service.

Reducing the Background Noise

By Hema Gandhi

"Your children are not your children. They are the sons and daughters of Life's longing for itself. They come through you but not from you. And though they are with you yet they belong not to you."

~ Kahlil Gibran

The feeling of complete and utter hopelessness that swallows you as you watch your child slowly disappear into autism is one that no mother would ever wish on anyone else. Your child is falling into an abyss that you can't even fathom in front of your eyes, yet there is nothing you can do to help him. You go to all the right people for help, but they give you conflicting information.

"It's because you had your second child too soon."

"He's just teething."

"Let's wait and see."

And the whole time, you know something is not right. That something is going completely and totally off track, and you feel like you cannot stop it.

My son, S., was 16 months old when his regression started. He was a happy-go-lucky child before. He had a handful of words, and he loved people. Anyone and everyone he encountered was someone to talk to, listen to, sing to him. But at 16 months, he started to withdraw into himself. It started with a simple illness. We assumed that he was just having a hard time recovering from his illness. He looked lost. He suddenly stopped understanding basic communication, even simple commands or requests. He was constantly climbing, burrowing into furniture and boxes, running nonstop. For lack of a better explanation, he wasn't comfortable in his own skin, and was making these odd gestures with his hands.

Clenching his fists.

And the sounds. Those odd, guttural sounds.

I remember a family member looking at him when he was two and saying he was just an "angry child," which he wasn't. But that brings us to the hardest part of this whole experience.

My husband and I not only had to deal with watching our child slip away from us, while dealing with a newborn baby in the house, but suddenly, we had to deal with a ton of criticism, as well. The criticism came from the very people we needed support from. In the process of trying to get S. diagnosed, I did a lot of research on the internet that made me believe he had autism. Had I not been searching, I would have never pinpointed so quickly what was wrong with my son, OR more importantly, that there was hope for children like S. to progress! Once I started asking about it, though, I was vilified for "trying to burden my child with a death sentence." Basically, I had Munchausen by proxy.

And once he was diagnosed, I was told everything from:

"It's your fault. You never nursed him," to "You didn't love him enough," to "You have bad energy, and your bad energy and vibes are giving S. these issues," to our all-time favorite "You didn't pray enough."

People that we had considered good friends suddenly were not around as much. At a time when Kishor and I needed a support system, we didn't know how to reach out for it.

There was definitely a period of soul searching for us. Did we indeed do something wrong? Was it my fault that S. had autism? Did we rush into this diagnosis that he would be stuck with for all of his life?

And then, we started Applied Behavior Analysis (ABA). I will be the first to admit that our foray into ABA was a bad experience. The agency was not the right fit for us. The lack of progress was disheartening and even more isolating than the diagnostic process. Then, shortly after S.'s fifth birthday, we started with an amazing new Board Certified Behavior Analyst (BCBA). There was, however, a stipulation that I find our own staff to ensure quality of care.

S. started to improve in leaps and bounds! But, along the way, we still faced difficulties. We realized that some aspects of ABA clashed with our very Indian attachment parent-oriented upbringing. Again, we faced judgement.

It was at this point that I finally had my moment of enlightenment. We hadn't done anything wrong. Unfortunately, any mental health diagnosis isn't discussed openly in our society. Add an additional layer of being an

Asian-American, and you have a whole new set of issues to deal with head on. The culture that my husband and I were raised in was not open to addressing mental health issues. We started to realize that autism was a brand new concept to the people advising us.

Maybe, just maybe, they were wrong.

Maybe, just maybe, we knew what we were doing.

We realized that it's easy to sit back and say that someone else is doing something wrong. But when it's your child's life and future on the line, you can't second guess yourself. You can only do the research, try to find answers from those you consider experts, and formulate a plan of action. You need to put on your blinders and noise-cancelling headphones and dive in. If you don't see progress, you need to speak up and make sure changes are made.

We realized that the background noise was with good intentions, but it was making us second-guess our every decision. And when we second-guessed ourselves, it was S. who suffered. So if you are reading this, and you are the background noise in an autism mom's life, PLEASE become the white noise for even a few minutes.

If you are an Asian-American autism mom like me, especially know this—there are so many of us out there. Reach out. Ask around. Don't hesitate. When one of our children progresses, it's as if a collective progressive step has been taken by all of our children. Don't let the hardest time of your life also be the loneliest. It is only in the last year that I have allowed myself the luxury of making time for myself and my friends. It is a life outside of S., and this is ok. You know who has benefited the most from this?

S.!

Reducing the Background Noise

Photographer: Hema Gandhi

Hema Gandhi is the mother of three wonderful kids. Her oldest, Sagar was diagnosed with ASD at 2.5 years, and their entire family has actively been involved in Sagar's therapy and development. Hema runs her own consulting business, focusing on Health Economics and Outcomes Research. She is currently pursuing her doctorate in the field of Population Health, with a focus on Applied Health Economics and Outcomes Research. She has published extensively in peer reviewed journals and has presented at various scientific conferences.

I Lost and Found Myself in Autism (and Other Labels)

Chou Hallegra

"And we know that God works all things for the good of those who love him, who have been called according to his purpose."

~ Romans 8:28

I am the proud and blessed mother of three amazing children. My oldest is 13, and my boys, who both have autism, are seven and five. The younger ones had multiple health issues already going on when we received the autism diagnosis. I felt as if I couldn't handle one more thing, and as a result, I lost myself in it all. Fortunately, I later found myself in what once looked like a huge mountain to climb.

I Lost and Found Myself in Autism (and Other Labels)

When my middle child was born, he was five days past his due date and quite a large baby. At nine pounds and four ounces, it wasn't easy to move him down the birth canal. I was pushing and pushing, but after trying so hard for many hours, he was turning blue. Doctors and nurses did everything they could to get him out alive. They pulled him out as quickly as they could, but he suffered a brachial plexus injury. He was paralyzed on the right side and was diagnosed with Erb's palsy a few hours after birth.

He spent a few days in the NICU. I was so sad going home without him, empty-handed and with a worried heart. I didn't know what the future held. Would he ever be able to move that arm, play ball, write . . . ? He also had an infection, and that just added to my list of worries.

Once he came home, we immediately started with Early Intervention services, so we now had a physical therapist coming to our home. A few days later, I realized that feeding this big baby was a challenge! He was hungry and wanted to eat but he couldn't latch on, which made breastfeeding difficult. I reached out to the lactation consultant at the hospital and went in for a consultation. She informed me that my child was tongue-tied. My first reaction was, "One more thing to worry about!"

We were referred for surgery. The outpatient procedure went well but didn't solve all of our problems. Afterward, my son could latch on, but then breast milk would dribble all over his neck. He was swallowing as quickly as the milk was flowing. I tried different baby bottles, with no success. We then added an occupational therapist to our Early Intervention team who informed me that my son's throat muscles were also affected by his birth injury. The muscles in his neck were weak, making it hard for him to suck. We started stem-electrotherapy, which helped stimulate the nerves that were impacted. The therapist also used different exercises and massages to teach him how to suck.

My middle son was about three months old when he was finally able to suck successfully. At four months, he started to move the fingers on his left hand and at six months, he was able to move half of his arm, from his elbow to his fingers. It was harder to move his forearm because the injury was at the shoulder, impacting the bones, joints, and muscles in that area. With physical and occupational therapy, he regained mobility in his right arm, although it can still be hard for him to carry heavy things.

I Lost and Found Myself in Autism (and Other Labels)

At eighteen months, I noticed that my son was not making many sounds like other kids his age. We added a special instructor to our team and she helped with overall development, especially language skills. Around twenty months old, my middle child had begun to verbally speak a few words. He could put three to four words together. We've worked so hard and had so many therapy sessions at home and in the community, as well as doctor appointments in different clinics, some as far as four hours away. This was hard work, but so worth it. I could see progress, and I was pleased by it.

Not long after, our world was shaken. My husband and I separated. My middle son began attending a local childcare center a few months prior. He was using a few words at the center, but when he was moved to the two-year-old class, he stopped talking in that school setting. He would talk in the car on the way there, but as soon as he passed through the double doors, he would be quiet for the rest of the day. When I picked him up, he would chatter all the way home and later into the night. He had developed selective mutism! Oh yes, yet one more thing to worry about!

Thankfully, the teacher in my son's new classroom was a very close family friend. She hung out with us on the weekends and even went on vacation with our family, but my son wouldn't talk to her inside the school. I knew there was more to this situation than just a two-year-old having trouble speaking. He had words, but something else was going on. I soon noticed that he was also having trouble with transitions. Moving from one activity to another would result in refusal or screaming or crying, especially if we were in a crowded place. Doing things in the community wasn't as fun as it used to be prior to these challenges.

Difficulties with transition intensified. At about 2.5 years old, sensory defensiveness also arose. My son didn't want me to hug him or touch him, especially if my hands were wet. He didn't want his food to touch, either! It needed to be separated on the plate or he wouldn't eat. He would refuse to wear certain clothing just because of the way it felt on his skin. He also became terrified of toilets, especially public restrooms that were so loud when you flushed them. He didn't like loud noises in general, which made it hard for our family to enjoy Christian concerts in the community as we did before.

During this time, our family was assigned a Clinical Social Worker through an Early Intervention program, who had some training in play therapy. She worked hard with my son and me. She not only helped him find the words for the emotions he was feeling, but also taught him how to play appropriately with toys and use his imagination. My son might still be a concrete thinker when it comes to everyday things, but his imagination runs wild when he is playing, and that's been such a joy to see. We also learned strategies to make transitions easier.

A few weeks before my son's third birthday, the Clinical Social Worker suggested that we obtain a psychological evaluation at one of the community mental health agencies. She had helped us tremendously during the short time that she was with us, and she wanted to make sure that we had the support and resources we needed once my son was discharged from Early Intervention at the age of three. The day after his third birthday, we went to a mental health agency in our community, and my son was diagnosed with autism. You guessed it—one more thing to worry about!

We had resources, and Early Intervention had made such a difference in my child's development, but now we had one more diagnosis to contend with, one more challenge to face. The biggest hurdle here was the fact that this diagnosis was long-term. This was not something that would just go away. By the age of three, my son had regained full mobility of his arm, and the effects of the Erb's palsy were very mild. He was still struggling with fine motor skills, but he was making great progress. The challenges that he previously faced were no longer affecting him as much, but autism was going to affect him for the rest of his life. That was a troublesome feeling for me as his mom. Little did I know that autism would change our lives for the better. Before I get to that, let me introduce you to my younger son.

The baby of our family was born 5.5 years ago. He was a little over six pounds, and experienced health issues immediately after birth. He had issues breathing, his heart was beating too fast, his potassium was high, and the medical staff and I both had a lot of questions. He and I stayed at the hospital a couple of days longer than planned.

The hospital staff asked me to take him to the pediatrician the day after we left the hospital. The pediatrician immediately sent us to the emergency room because my son was jaundiced and his potassium was unstable. That was the beginning of what felt like never-ending trips to the emergency room and hospitals. I was informed that my son's high potassium was causing his rapid heart rate.

I Lost and Found Myself in Autism (and Other Labels)

During the first eighteen months of my youngest son's life, we spent more time in the emergency room, specialty clinics, and urgent care facilities than I had in the three decades that I had lived that far. We had many hospital stays, as well. During one of those hospital stays, we found out that my son had Klinefelter syndrome, G6PD deficiency, and adrenal insufficiency. At 12 months, he was diagnosed with eosinophilic esophagitis, and at 18 months, he received a mild cerebral palsy diagnosis. The autism diagnosis came at 2.5, and other diagnoses such as asthma, pica, and conduct disorder, were added later on.

I now had SEVERAL things to worry about!

His future was so uncertain in the beginning of his life journey. The first time we almost lost him was when he was only three weeks old. Like his older brother, he also received Early Intervention services, in addition to having a complex team of medical professionals. At one time we were seeing ten different pediatric specialists: a geneticist, neurologist, orthopedist, allergist, pulmonologist, gastroenterologist, endocrinologist, nutritionist, urologist, developmental pediatrician, as well as a physician from rehabilitation medicine. I thank God that he is alive and that his conditions are well managed.

Caring for children with special needs and/or chronic health issues is one of the hardest things I have ever done in my life. Some of the specialists that we see are over two hours away from our home, but they have been such a blessing in our lives that it is worth the trip. At times, though, all the therapy sessions and doctor appointments leave me depleted physically, mentally, emotionally, and financially.

By the time that my youngest child was diagnosed with autism, I found myself caring for a 4.5-year-old and a 2.5-year-old with multiple diagnoses.

I knew how to take care of them, but I had forgotten how to take care of me.

It was no surprise that I lost myself in my role as a caregiver. I wasn't just a mom. I was the case manager, the resource coordinator, the therapist, the driver, and the human resource manager for all the people working with all of my kids. There was no time or energy left for me, or so I thought.

I became so stressed out. I did not get enough sleep at night, nor was I eating adequately. Most days, I didn't remember if I ate or when I ate. My health took a toll, and I realized that something had to change. I had to start taking care of myself, or there would be no one to take care of my children. I needed to find balance.

I had previously left a job because of my youngest son's medical needs because I had to stay home with him. I knew that was the best thing for him and for our family at the time, and I loved being a mom first. However, this also added to my loss of identity. I was already not doing the things I used to enjoy because I had neither the time nor the energy to pursue them, and now I was no longer using my skills and talents. My work gave me a sense of purpose and accomplishment outside of my role as a mom.

Autism may have been the straw that broke the camel's back, but I started losing myself way before that diagnosis. How do I begin to take care of myself? How would I find myself? How would I enjoy myself and life again while caring for my children and their needs? It wasn't an easy quest, yet it was an important one. It was necessary.

I decided to break the isolation first. This world of caring for kids with special needs was not meant to be walked alone. I started connecting to other parents who were going through similar things. I contacted Parent to Parent and was matched with other families with similar diagnoses. I also connected with other caregivers on social media, especially in Facebook groups. I attended different events for families of children with autism and other diagnoses, and that introduced me to The Special Kids Network and groups led by the Autism Society. I was no longer alone. I had a tribe of people who have been there and who are living what I'm going through. I learned from them and provided support in return.

When I felt supported, it became easier to make self-care a priority in my own life. The more I connected with others, the more I found out about resources that could help my family, such as respite and home health services. The more I was connected to services, the more I felt comfortable letting trained individuals care for my children for a limited time so I could take a nap, take a shower, or even make my own doctor's appointments. The more I took care of myself, the better I felt physically, emotionally, and mentally and the happier I felt. Taking care of myself made me a better mom, as well, because it helped me be fully present with my kids. Life didn't have to be a chore anymore.

I eventually became a mental health and disability consultant, and most of the work I do around disability is for people with autism and those who care for them. A lot of the people who helped us along the way became partners and colleagues. When my middle child was just six months old, I joined Early Intervention's Parents as Partners in Professional Development (P3D). Although I wasn't involved as much at first, for the past four years, I've been such a big part of what they do.

Through P3D, I have presented at the National Autism Conference in State College for the past four years, trained other families around the LifeCourse tools, and even served on a panel discussion on how Supports Coordinators can be more culturally competent. I was also the parent co-chair for my Local Interagency Council (LLC) which expanded my network and supports. When the Office of Developmental Programs wanted to train family members on Person-Centered Thinking, I jumped on the wagon. For the past four years, I have been teaching Person-Centered Thinking across the state of Pennsylvania. I also started my own consulting, counseling, and coaching business after my sons were diagnosed.

Once again, I am able to use my skills and talents to make a difference, and autism has been such a big part of it. I love what I do, and my kids' diagnoses are what introduced me to this field. My last straw became a blessing not just to my family but to many others. My kids get to be part of all of this in such a positive way! They go with me to conferences and trainings as much as possible. I also get to share their stories during my trainings, which in turn helps so many others.

I'm happy to report that my boys are doing well. We still have our challenges, but they're so mild compared to where we were before. Both of my boys are advocating for their own needs. They love to play with other children and are thriving in school and in the community. My middle child is going into second grade and no longer needs physical, occupational, or speech therapy. He loves to play sports and cook, and he gets to do both of those things in our community through sports camps and cooking classes.

My youngest child gives the best hugs ever and loves to make people laugh. He just finished preschool and already knows all his letters and colors, and he can even count up to thirty. He can write his name and figure out the hardest puzzles. As a family, we have so much fun exploring together. We love to go to the pool, state parks, the creek, playgrounds, library, festivals, community fairs, beach, and other towns. My sons have instilled in me a sense of adventure and have made their sister into the most caring young lady we know.

I Lost and Found Myself in Autism (and Other Labels)

Autism is not the end of the world, and it should not be the end of your life or your child's life either. Your kids can thrive in spite of autism. You, as a parent, can thrive both personally and professionally through your child's diagnosis. I wish I had someone to tell me those things earlier on. Now, I get to tell you. You have someone (me!) telling you to live on, to continue to pursue your interests and passions and to envision a bigger and better life for your children, despite the difficult season that you are in.

Chou Hallegra

Photographer: Hope Naysha

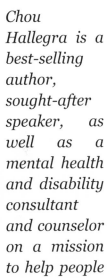

Chou Hallegra is a best-selling author, sought-after speaker, as well as a mental health and disability consultant and counselor on a mission to help people to help people rise above their circumstances and live fulfilling lives. Chou is originally from Brazzaville, Congo. She resides in South Central Pennsylvania with her family. Find out more about Chou and her work at www.graceandhopeconsulting.com.

Cultivating A Spectrum of Possibility
(While Consuming Copious Amounts of Coffee)

Catherine A. Hughes

"I don't need an inspirational quote. I need coffee."

~ Random coffee lover

Ok, so maybe you aren't a coffee drinker. I'm not judging. Maybe I am a little, alright, you got me. Perhaps your preference is tea. Or maybe you drink water (and maybe you can poke me to increase my own healthy hydration). Me, I need my coffee, and I need plenty of it.

Let's face it—no matter what hurdles are before you, you need coping mechanisms to effectively manage your stress, motivation to move forward, and experiences that simply give you a reason to smile. It just so happens that one of mine is coffee, coffee, and more coffee.

Like the beautiful, powerful, exquisite women who grace the pages of this book, I draw on not just my daily caffeine jolt, but strong conviction from deep down in my soul to continue to create a path not just for myself and for my son Christian, but also for individuals and family members who have been impacted by autism as we have that I am so blessed to support through my calling (not career, but *calling*).

I remember exactly what I was wearing on April 19, 2001—an orange polo shirt, khaki capris, brown suede boots, and a matching brown suede button down blazer. It was seemingly another day, another doctor's appointment. This time, it was with our endocrinologist. Following that appointment, my family tried to enjoy a meal before I had to head to work. That day, my parents (who helped raise my son, as I was a young single mother) and I were told that Christian's tantrums, lack of language, and peculiar behaviors couldn't just be a "boy thing" and that we needed to continue to seek answers.

I never made it home to call for help or make any appointments.

" . . . you are under arrest for terroristic threats, endangering the welfare of a minor, and simple assault on your son."

This statement was made by an officer who never read my rights. I was arrested and then jailed for four days in downtown Pittsburgh after patrons and the manager of a local restaurant watched me trying to calm my son during a meltdown and then remove him from the premises. They interpreted what they saw as child abuse, not once thinking "maybe this mother needs some help" or "why is this child struggling so much."

Child abuser. The people standing around the restaurant lobby while I was in handcuffs repeated those words in my ear, over and over again. I can still hear them if I sit silently enough.

Fast forward 6 weeks ...

". . . Pervasive Developmental Disorder, NOS." Dr. Newman said to me,

"This is something he can grow out of, right? I can get him help. At least he's not on the spectrum. That's a relief. It's not my fault."

"Cathy . . ." he said gently. "No, this is not your fault. It's nobody's fault. But PDD-NOS . . . it is on what we call 'the spectrum.' Cathy, your son has a form of autism."

At that moment, I felt everything around me disappear, like I was sitting in an empty white room with endless walls and time and space. I felt great confusion setting in, incredible sadness for my son's future, immense anger at my pediatrician for not believing me when I asked for help as I insisted something wasn't right, and guilt for feeling a slight twinge of relief.

Inspired, influenced, and impacted by more people than I can count—clinicians, teachers, doctors, and people **JUST LIKE YOU** (and yes, also more trips to Dunkin' and Starbucks than I can count and willingly admit), we have blazed a trail and we have defied many odds.

If you have ever felt, or still feel, as if your loved one's diagnosis is your fault, I want you to STOP what you are doing right now, look in a mirror, and say out loud, "This is not my fault. This is who he (she) is."

I also need you to say, "My loved one is not broken. They are not defective. They have a different way of being. It is up to me to accept, act, advocate, and always love."

And add this, "My loved one is a gift—maybe their struggles are not, but their talents and their being are. And together, we will change the world."

Please, say these affirmations until you believe them.

There's a quote floating in the autism community that goes something like this: "This wasn't the trip I was expecting, but I love my tour guide."

Christian's journey through intensive years of ABA treatment, outpatient therapies, nutritional and medical interventions, and schooling has not just led him to a place of abundance that at one point seemed so uncertain, but also propelled me to create a powerful and rewarding career where I can graciously give back some of what was given to my family.

My son, as I wrote this chapter, just turned 21. With support from our "aumazing" village and his own fierce determination, he is a high school honor graduate who achieved scholarships and community accolades. He has held part time jobs, and is currently seeking a position helping the elderly by volunteering his time at a local facility and working with a job coach to hone in on his skills. He's also learning to drive. Oh heavens yes, mama needs plenty of coffee when Christian is behind the wheel of the new Jeep.

As for me, I am blessed to serve as the Director of Family Support and Community Engagement at Achieving True Self, an organization that provides home and community services (primarily ABA at the time this was written) to families. I am also the founder of The Caffeinated Advocate, a blog (and brand perhaps, all to be determined in time) that allows me yet another avenue to share our living, breathing story with others and bless them as I have been called to do.

"How do you do it (besides several cups of coffee a day)?" I don't have a one-size-fits-all answer for you. There is no secret sauce that is going to provide you with the recipe for you or your loved ones. The spectrum is simply that—a spectrum—and though we all walk on the same planet, our paths sometimes run parallel and won't always intersect.

What I can tell you is to be gentle with yourself as you learn, as you cope, and as you find your way through the tunnel and seek the light. I promise you, it is there. Some days it is hard to see. I would be lying if I said all of our days were filled with sunshine and rainbows.

Cultivating a Spectrum of Possibility

They aren't. The lightning still strikes, the thunder roars, and the rain still pours.

But I promise you—support, resources, and ultimately hope for tomorrow always exists. Put in the work, follow your heart and gut unapologetically, and you will discover rewards.

To you, dear reader, I salute (with what else . . . my mug) and toast to your family's future, with incredible love and light.

Catherine A. Hughes

Photographer: Jackie Carlantonio

Hailing from southeast of Pittsburgh, PA, in a small town recently dubbed as "the most boring town in Pennsylvania," *Catherine is an innovative storyteller and community strategist employed in leadership at Achieving True Self. Inspired by raising her son with autism, now 21, she has built a career providing comprehensive support and passionate advocacy for children, families and their surrounding communities. She is a servant leader who cultivates relationships with grace and grit to create, enhance, and promote services and programs that transform lives. She maintains a blog and social media platforms, called The Caffeinated Advocate, and is currently working on several collaborations, as well as her first solo publication, Imprisoned No More.*

My Little

Donna P. Lund

"The only thing I do know is that my life is my story and I want it to read the best way possible."

~ Donna Lund

Writing this chapter is a trip down memory lane. I remember the good, the bad, and the memories that lay somewhere in between. I have many memories of my older children—Nikki, Donny, and Catie—together and then singular memories of my baby Brian. For some reason, not much overlap exists: almost like a chunk of time is missing from my psyche.

Most of my memories of Brian start when he entered kindergarten, other than vivid memories of carrying him around everywhere (best arm toning exercise ever). Truth be told, my life was in chaos and I was trying to hide that chaos behind a big smile and the false projection of normalcy. Brian was born in December of Donny's first grade year and that is precisely when Donny's struggles were taking on a life of their own and taking over our family. His delays were becoming more and more obvious, and I could see the kids moving forward and away from him. I had visions of how his future was going to look as school progressed and I didn't like what I saw. My role as his mom was taking on many facets for which I was not in any way prepared. I spent a lot of time trying to explain his behavior, but that was a very difficult task when I didn't understand it myself.

On top of all of this, I had a preschooler and a fourth grader. A full plate for sure and to say I was overwhelmed would have been an understatement. How could I possibly, with any grace and confidence, be a good mother to my fourth child when I was consumed by thoughts and fears of whether he also would be autistic? I just didn't feel equipped. I think my brain went into self-defense mode and created some hazy spots in my memory.

Many autism moms have probably experienced something similar as part of their initiation into the least sought after but fastest growing sorority around: the sorority of Isolated

My Little

Autism Moms, or "IAM." I recently had the chance to act as a "big sister" to a new initiate .

My "little" was going through a very hard time as she was trying to adapt to her new life as an autism mom. She was trying to manage her family, her son's education, and her broken heart. It was an awful lot to process, and it brought back to me all the conflicting emotions I experienced when I was in her shoes. I went over to her house to offer her some much needed support. I could not offer her solutions to her situation because I have not figured that out in my own world. That was not the intent of my visit.

Like a good big, I offered her my unconditional friendship and told her I am here for her. I told my little that nothing can faze or shock me, and nothing needs explained to me. I told her that I would never think less of her as her child spirals out of control, because I have been there more times than I care to remember. I shared with her some stories so she would know that I am qualified to be her big.

I will take her under my wing, show her the ropes and hope that my life experiences can serve as a rough road map for her. Since my real sister died, I have missed being a big sister, and here was a chance to help someone. True gratification comes from within, and helping this young mom actually filled my heart more than hers. Maybe helping her will help me make sense of all the pain I've endured over the past 20 years and give me a broader purpose.

I want to be for her the person I desperately needed 20 years ago.

When I left her house, I cried. I saw pieces of both my sons in her beautiful, non-verbal little boy. I saw my younger self in her—the younger self who just wanted her worries to be like the other moms. I wanted to be thinking about whether my son was going to make the travel baseball team or be invited to the birthday party. I wanted to sit through a presentation at open house in the fall and have the curriculum actually pertain to him. It was not much fun pretending it did while holding back tears. I eventually stopped going.

I desperately wanted things to be different. Like I did many years ago, this young mom now faces much more complicated worries, and she recognizes the road ahead is going to be rough. She has no idea of the expectations that will be placed upon her as she is expected to be an expert on behavior, communication, special education all while managing what feels like an impossible system. I felt her pain and witnessed her confusion. Mostly, I saw her unwavering love and devotion to her son and the desperation she felt trying to manage his world and also that of her typically developing little girl. Through my tears, however, I thought, "what a lucky little boy."

They will be okay, because she will see to it. She will most likely keep readjusting her dreams like I did. My little can do this. She will surprise herself.

The autism journey will no doubt separate you from some of your friends because circumstances will demand it. While you are spending hours in weekly therapy and feel lost in a daze of worry, a whole new social dynamic is developing without you. Sadly, it is just the way it is sometimes, and you need to let yourself grieve any loss. Shutting people out is very easy to do as your path takes you further from the norm and, in the long run, will only make things more difficult. I promise you, good people are out there and they will appear when you least expect them. Or the right people could have been at your side all along, but you were too brokenhearted to see it.

Dig deep, and say "goodbye" to the life you choreographed for yourself. Embrace the present day. In doing so, you will allow yourself to meet others, and in my case some of the most caring and supportive people I know. The thread I'm trying to weave here is that you can always find a friend. Thankfully, someone has always appeared in my life at the darkest times and pulled me through.

Obviously, the sorority of "IAM" doesn't exist in a formal sense, but quietly it has evolved and is very real. All autism moms are welcome and its mission is to let younger moms know they will not only survive, they will thrive! Admittedly, I entered the world of special needs kicking and screaming. However, even with all of the complicated challenges I can't envision my life any other way. After many years, I have found peace. You will see profound beauty in small successes and love more than you thought possible.

A few nights ago, my daughter Catie was upset and crying. Brian came in from the other room, wiped away her tears and gave her a hug and a kiss. It was spontaneous and real and profound and beautiful. He would not leave her side until she was ok.

It sums up everything I have been trying to say in a simple gesture. It was a priceless moment that only an initiate to the "IAM" sorority can experience. It was a moment that reconciled me to all the struggles, doubts, and fears imposed on me as an autism mom. You also will have such moments. Know that you can do this.

For every little, there is a big, and we will get through this together.

Donna Lund

Photographer:
Jackie Carlantonio

Donna is a wife, mother of four, and loving advocate from Pittsburgh, PA. Both of her sons have ASD. Her contribution to the autism community in her early years focused on fundraising, and she raised over $150,000 for Autism Speaks. In 2011, the Lund family was featured in a documentary, The Family Next Door. The film's mission was to illustrate the emotional impact of autism on families, and its influence has led to speaking engagements that focus on Donna's message of compassion. She has been invited to speak at local universities with special education teachers as well as at high schools (including annually at Mt. Lebanon School District as part of their curriculum) to promote professional development. Donna was a speaker at the Robert Morris University Educational Conference and a guest panelist for Representative Dan Miller's Disability Summit.

My Little

In 2018, she launched her blog, Labeled to Lunderful.

How Will You Cast Your Stone?

Patti McCloud

"I alone cannot change the world, but I can cast a stone across the waters to create many ripples."

~ Mother Teresa

In this journey of autism, we're all doing the best we can to provide meaningful lives for our children.

The truth is that my son, Jordan, was perfectly and wonderfully made by God. We're just trying to catch up to him. He is a huge presence in our lives—a smiling, laughing, goofy blessing.

Jordan can light up room with his smile. He loves to make us laugh. He has an endearing spirit that draws teachers and aides and care workers to him. For the most part, he is pretty easy-going. He loves to hang out with his sister, his dad, and his big extended family and friends. He can spend hours navigating YouTube and flipping from site to site without ever having typed a letter.

It's easy to show or talk about only the good. We've been doing it since Jordan was born. "We're good!" "Jordan's good!"

But I'd be lying if I didn't tell you that on some days it's harder to find the blessing than others. It's easy to control what we let you see on the surface. It's hard to be vulnerable and share the tough stuff. There are many days when I feel like I've failed Jordan in some way. I think to myself, "If we'd only done more therapy," or "tried one more time with the diet." The list goes on and on. You see, Jordan does not yet have the overcomer success story.

Jordan needs help with all daily living skills, such as showering, dressing, and some assistance at mealtime. At 22 years old, Jordan is not completely toilet-trained. Jordan has a short attention span and must constantly be redirected to the task at hand, which makes it hard to learn vocational skills. When he's frustrated, he hits or destroys things. He has no concept of safety or danger and must be constantly watched.

JORDAN DOES NOT SPEAK. NOT A SINGLE WORD.

He can't tell us what is wrong when he's hurting or sick, he can't tell us when he's bored or annoyed or frustrated. We've never heard him say "I love you." Not even once. On the rare occasion that he cries, it is absolutely heart shattering as we try to navigate what the real issue is and what he is trying to communicate to us.

Some days seem very long. When you are exhausted from lack of sleep and getting pinched or pushed and you're watching your beautiful child bite himself in frustration, it's hard to see the blessing.

When you sit in yet another IEP meeting at school and hear the same goals with just a little bit of progress from year to year, it's like a punch in the chest every time, and it's really hard to see the blessing.

When you petition the court for guardianship of your child and they so easily agree because it's very clear that Jordan will need us to make decisions on his behalf for the rest of his life, it's hard to see the blessing.

How Will You Cast Your Stone

When you look ahead and see so little opportunity for your child, it's terrifying. Jordan has been in treatment and therapy since he was three years old, yet as an adult, he functions more like a gigantic three year old.

But even on the darkest, most frustrating days, when the only thing you want to do is just close your eyes and go to sleep so you can wake up and start again, there is hope. We have hope that tomorrow will be better, that we can make tomorrow better, that tomorrow will bring new mercies. We have to hold on to hope for a better future.

After 22 years in this journey, I'm finally learning to trust my gut and to stop second-guessing myself. I've learned that not every treatment works for every child. You can pour your heart and soul (and a whole lot of money) into a treatment or diet that might not be the answer for your son or daughter. I've also learned that, sometimes, things are meant to happen in their own time and that it's ok to go back and revisit something that didn't work in the past. Sometimes quality of life—for everyone—is what is most important. I've learned that the learning and the skills development doesn't end, and just because they couldn't do it before, doesn't mean they can't learn it later. I'm getting way better at seeing the blessings.

Jordan is so smart. He loves to be with his peers. He is learning new skills every day and new ways to show what he knows. He has a huge crush on a girl named Rosa. He loves to tease his sister and hug us when we've been away from him. He loves to watch YouTube clips and Steelers videos and attend Pirates games. I have no doubt that he understands everything that we say to him and about him. He communicates with no words and he keeps finding ways to show us what he needs or what he knows.

Just like everyone, Jordan deserves a meaningful, purposeful life—whatever that looks like. He deserves to live as independently as possible surrounded by his peers. He deserves to find some type of competitive employment. None of that will be easy. He's going to need help and lifelong supports.

And he's not alone.

Over 70% of adults with autism are not employed or under-employed. There are tens of thousands of adults on waiting lists for waiver dollars that will allow them to access support and housing. Many adults with autism, even those with higher level skills, require support and services throughout their lifetimes to ensure success.

Legendary broadcaster and Hall of Fame football player Frank Gifford passed away a few years ago, and his wife gave a beautiful tribute to Frank regarding his faith. Regardless of all of the awards and accolades that Frank received in his life, he was most touched by a trip he took to the Holy Land and the Brook of Elah, which is where David slayed the giant Goliath.

David was able to slay the giant because of the faith he had in his God. Frank brought home a stone and he kept it in his trophy room, and he would take people in there and show them that stone. He would often give stones to important people in his life and challenge them by asking them how they would cast their stone in life? How would they affect others? What was their part in the bigger picture?

Autism is our Goliath!

Special education budgets are strained, there is a lack of providers for therapeutic services, and thousands of young adults are aging out the education system and will need support, care, places to live, and places to work.

What's your part of the puzzle? How will you cast your stone? How will you help provide that hope to families? How will we provide what our children need? It will take a huge village to help provide a meaningful, purposeful life for the Jordans of the world.

And so I ask you, if this resonates with you, please share your story. It's important and unique and it needs to be heard. If there is one thing that I've learned after years of advocating for Jordan at both a local and national level, it's that legislators, policymakers, funders, and county officials really don't know what our lives are like. And they really do want to know.

Show and tell them what you go through on a daily basis. Share your successes and your frustrations. If you can take your child to visit them at an event or at their local office, do that. Are you afraid that your child might be disruptive or exhibit some strange or aggressive behaviors? Let them see your loved ones for who they are. Are you afraid they won't be able to read your documents because your child flooded the kitchen counter when you were in the shower? Trust me, that makes a big impact. If you don't bring them, that's ok, too, but bring a picture with you.

Feeling so overwhelmed that you can't fathom getting to someone's office to share your story? We've all been there. Send a text or email and be heard. There are many national and local organizations that make it very easy for you to fill in your information and hit send. You can even attend events where you can share your story. Cast your stone!

It's easy to get discouraged. It's easy to feel sorry for yourself some days. It's ok to cry in the car or the shower and let all that frustration out. But don't stay there too long. And don't waste that frustration and anger, use it for the greater good. Share your story!

Find a local organization, and subscribe to their email lists. Find parents that are going through similar issues and make a point to get together in person or even in a Facebook group. I used to meet with a group of parents while our kids attended social groups together. Some of the best laughs I've ever had are with other parents as we share the absurdity of our situations along with all of the really interesting advice we've heard over the years. Those groups will be your lifeline to learning about services and treatments and funding sources.

Then, find a group of friends who have no connection to autism and make it a point to get together with them. If someone offers help, take it. Find a way to get respite. We all worry about caretakers not understanding or being able to effectively care for our child. Remember though, you need to take care of yourself before you can take care of someone else.

Finally, please have compassion and empathy for all who are on this journey with us, respecting everyone's choices. Don't bash other organizations. Find your passion and what you want to support and let others do the same. We are all trying to do the best we can. We all have different experiences and are seeking different things.

Oh, and share your story. You have no idea who you might touch, and in your sharing, you will encourage others to share. Autism can be a lonely journey, but it can also introduce you to some incredible individuals along the way.

After 20 years in this autism game, I know that change is slow. But our stories do make a difference and will create a better world.

Share your story. Find your tribe. Count your blessings. Cast your stone.

Photographer: Jackie Carlantonio

Patti McCloud and family have served in fundraising and advocacy efforts since 2000. She has served as the family teams and corporate fundraising chair and as co-chair of the Pittsburgh Walk in 2004 and 2005. In 2008, she participated on a panel at the Autism Speaks National Leadership Retreat. In 2009 and 2010, Patti served as community advocacy chair in Pennsylvania. She helped secure Act 62 in Pennsylvania and the passage of the federally funded Department of Defense Bill. She has chaired Dress It Up Blue and Chefs Create Pittsburgh, raising hundreds of thousands of dollars for Autism Speaks. She has been an active Board Member of their Pittsburgh Chapter serving in various capacities.

Patti McCloud

Patti is employed with Pressley Ridge as their Family Support Coordinator. She lives in Mars, PA, with her son, Jordan, diagnosed with autism and intellectual disability, and her daughter, Nicole, who attends the University of Kentucky.

Raising Authentic and "Ausome" Brothers

Sarah Parks

"There's no person in the whole world like you. And I like you just the way you are."

~ Fred Rogers

"You aren't spending enough time with him."

"Nothing is wrong with him."

"He'll grow out of it."

Colby's delayed speech made me want to reach out for Early Intervention and developmental therapy. As he grew older, he was still not making eye contact, responding to his name, or talking. I filled out an autism screening survey at the pediatrician's office at his two-year checkup which came back negative. This was my first child. I was listening to the doctor.

He would constantly cry and scream in public restrooms while I changed his diaper which I found so strange because he didn't fuss at home when being changed. There was a lot of rocking back and forth, humming loudly, and some self-injurious behaviors. There were no reasons for these outbursts that I could see.

"What is happening? What is wrong?" I would ask myself and cry.

I felt like a bad mom.

I felt helpless.

The only way to console him was to leave wherever we were. I felt so embarrassed because I didn't know how to soothe my crying child. Did people think I was a horrible and abusive mother?

Going out with friends became nearly impossible. I couldn't socialize because Colby was hyper and got into everything. Even to this day, he is either sleeping or going 100 mph.

He would not listen to me at all. "Why can't I parent?" I would ask. People would say to me, "Kids will be kids. Stop complaining."

I didn't feel like I was complaining. I knew parenting was going to be hard, but not *THIS* hard. I had been around many children before having any of my own, and I had never seen so much defiance and screaming from one child at one time. I saw other people far worse off than me, and their children didn't act out like this. "What am I doing wrong?" I would continue to ask myself, time and time again.

The invites to hang out with friends dwindled.

I felt alone.

I felt depressed.

I began to avoid socializing, and isolated myself from social gatherings altogether—as if those friends hadn't already isolated themselves from me.

His Early Intervention therapists suggested that I take him to the local Child Development Unit for a psychological evaluation. The first available appointment was in six months.

I sat there, pregnant with our second child, when the psychologist came into the room and said "Your son has autism."

Two months later, I gave birth to our second child—a boy, who would later be diagnosed with autism as well.

Some people view the initial autism diagnosis as horrible, but I didn't. Immediately after receiving the first autism diagnosis, I went home and read a lot on the subject. It helped me understand my son better. Being given the diagnosis answered a lot of questions that I had about his behaviors and why "typical parenting" wasn't working.

Now that we had a diagnosis, we could access the help and support that Colby needed so badly. The diagnosis didn't change who he was, but now I would know how to help him. None of my friends at the time had a child with autism, so I felt completely alone, isolated, and lost. After the diagnosis, the friends who had written us off didn't come back around. Even some family members were skittish about it.

"Nothing is wrong with him. You just don't discipline enough!" This was the time when I needed support and help. I was getting very little from very few.

In time, I made new friends with fellow "autism moms" from the outpatient therapy waiting rooms, at the special preschool, and through local autism organizations. If I hadn't met them, I would still feel alone, isolated, and lost. These families have gotten me through some rough times, and vice versa. I am happy to say that some of them have become my best friends.

I couldn't have been happier when one of the Therapeutic Support Staff (TSS) assigned to our son shared that she could teach him sign language. Colby was still nonverbal at the time, so that was a huge help. Miss Nicki was the angel we needed. I will be forever grateful to her for helping my child and me learn how to communicate with one another. I am also grateful to Variety - The Children's Charity (Pittsburgh, PA) for giving Tyler, my youngest, the gift of voice by presenting him with his very own Augmentative and Assisted Communication (AAC) device to communicate his wants and needs.

I fear that some people think I throw "autism" around to get personal attention. I know I'm not alone in that.

That is far from the truth.

I am trying to educate others and spread awareness to the public and to loved ones. I talk about the highs, the lows, and everything in between. "Being a parent is hard for anyone" is something that was said to me that has stuck. Yes, I agree it is hard, but add many significant needs and adaptations into the mix!

Having two children, one with zero words and one with limited reciprocal conversation skills, I have to be very vigilant. I've been called a "helicopter mom," and I don't think that I am. I let them have fun and explore. I follow them around to ensure their safety because they have no concept of danger.

One of my biggest fears is for them to come around the corner bleeding or seriously injured. They wouldn't be able to tell me how it happened. So how would I find out? An ER doctor would ask, "How did this happen?" and I would have to say, "I don't know."

YEAH. That would make me Mother of the Year.

Another fear of mine is that one or both of them will wander off. When I discovered that the county we live in has a program to assist with easing that fear, I was overcome with joy. The program is called *Project Lifesaver*. Once you enroll, you are given a tracking device to wear either on your wrist or your ankle. If the individual should go missing, someone would just call 911 and provide their identifying number, and the search would begin immediately.

Throughout the day, I literally have to be in two places at the same time almost constantly. One child is screaming, crying, and bleeding all over the place, and while I am tending to that, his sibling is letting out blood-curdling screams because the screaming of his brother is hurting his head. The "typical" parent would say from across the room, "put that down" or "don't do that." For my children, I have to physically go over and redirect them hand over hand because they do not respond to verbal commands. One needs deep pressure and squeezes while the other may not be feeling well and wants to be cuddled.

It is really hard to get anything done throughout the day. It is also very hard to discipline them. I often fight with myself about WHAT to even discipline them about. Are they acting out because of their autism, or are they just being a . . . kid? I have two children, both with autism. What is "typical behavior"? I don't even know.

Loud screaming makes them scream back in return, because it hurts their ears and startles them. Let's say that Tyler is crying in pain or anger. Colby then starts screaming along because Tyler's screaming is bothering HIM. We have noise cancelling headphones for both boys, but they don't help with all noises.

It's like my life is a battle, not an intentional one, but one nonetheless.

The more I read about autism and heard stories shared from my friends, the more I understood the reasons why my boys behave the way they do. Our lives changed after the diagnoses, but I now know what help they need to be their best selves. I know what I need to do, to say, and how to act toward them.

I am so proud of both of my boys. They have come so far with hard work. I just hope that spreading of awareness never stops.

These boys are my world, and I wouldn't change them. They are who they are.

Raising Authentic and "Ausome" Brothers

Photographer:
Little Daisy Photography LLC

Sarah Parks, devoted wife and mother of two "ausome brothers" was born, raised, and still resides in Pittsburgh, PA. An avid scrapbooking fanatic, Sarah grew up with a spark for helping others. She started young with Brownies in the second grade, became an alter server, joined her church youth group, enrolled at her local volunteer fire company as a teen, and assisted at a vacation bible school. Sarah has always followed a calling to serve and "be a good neighbor." Compassionate, giving, loyal, and kind, this "ausome mom" fundraises for walks supporting local grassroots organizations, is engaged with her school's PTA, and facilitates connections to create awareness efforts, including within her children's school district. Sarah is on a mission to share resources and experiences with anyone

*in need or who will listen—and while she's at it,
she will keep you smiling and laughing.*

Who's There When It's Time to Blow Out the Candles?

Holly Teegarden

"The greatest gift that you can give to others is the gift of unconditional love and acceptance."

~ Brian Tracy

One of the feelings that you will find threaded through any autism family stories is the sense of isolation. It's common, and sometimes the isolation feels like it will swallow you whole. Your child is different, and for many kids and even their parents, they don't know how to accept or handle it. My daughter in her own nature isolated herself and still does. It's her way of coping with things. It's not that she's unhappy; it's just that she feels more comfortable being alone.

As a parent of a child on the spectrum, you also deal with feelings of isolation. You can't really talk about the issues that you're tackling with your child with parents of typical children. If I were to tell my girlfriends when Sarah was young about echolalia (repeating what someone else said without being asked to) or her obsessions with order, they would have felt sorry for me, and that's not what I wanted. I would rather just deal with it alone.

Advocating for your child can become a full-time job, which leaves little to no time for socializing, even with your own spouse. You're living in a world where your child is isolating themselves for their own survival, and you're doing it at the same time too. There is no greater example of this than with birthday parties.

The dreaded birthday parties.

My daughter is 11, soon to be 12, and she has probably been invited to about 10 classmate parties total.

Maybe.

For years, the number was at zero. Not one classmate. Can you imagine? As a parent, you want to shield them from the harsh realities of the world where they might feel unwanted or not loved by their peers. And what would stink is I knew that my daughter knew about the parties going on around her. She would tell me that everyone is going to this person's party.

Everyone, but her.

Part of me wanted to call the parents and shout, "WTF, people?" I get that my kid might talk to herself or blurt things out but still, have a damn heart.

If you're reading this and have a child in elementary school, please do me a favor, and invite everyone to your next birthday party. Don't leave kids out just because they're "different."

To combat this void of not being invited to other parties, we would make OUR birthday parties BIG! When my new husband got on the "big party train" he was like, "You do this every. single. year?" Yes sir, like a boss, I said.

I'm sure other parents were probably thinking, what are these people, moneybags? They are always throwing some elaborate event that was fun, and everyone would be invited. I literally didn't care what the cost was when it came to her party. I know that seems nuts to many people. Our hope was that they would see

Sarah as just a "normal kid," and the parents of her peers would perhaps be empathetic and explain to their kids that different is okay. I'm sure some of you just read this paragraph and thought I was trying to buy friends for my child.

Yes, yes I was. It's sad that I felt I needed to do that.

I do want to say that Sarah, in time, did start to receive party invitations. God bless neighbors and friends of our family, because she finally was invited to their children's birthday parties! The invites weren't mercy invites, but invites from those who truly understood Sarah and enjoyed being around her.

I want to share with you a little bit about the first birthday party that she ever attended. She doesn't remember, but I remember this day vividly.

It was 2011. Sarah was 4 years old and recently diagnosed with PDD-NOS. We got her into music and movement classes with this sweet mom whose son was also in the class. During the class, Sarah enjoyed the music but made very little eye contact, didn't speak, and kept to herself. We didn't realize just how different she was until we started putting her into group situations like this. Imagine our surprise when Sarah got an invite for the son's 5th birthday party. The party was at a local park. Low key. We thought, "This is going to be great! She loves going to our park and always has fun.

When we got there, Sarah didn't want to play with anyone. Or speak to anyone. She would sit alone in different areas or wander toward the woods, away from the party. My ex-husband and I had to stay vigilant watching her and not socialize with the other parents the whole time.

Remember when I talked about isolation at the beginning of this chapter. This is it folks, slapping you in the face: parents focused on their child, not talking to any other parents, and the child lacking social and verbal skills themselves.

I remember talking to my ex-husband as we watched Sarah that day. It hit us just how different she was from the rest of the kids. It was gut-wrenching to watch her—and watching ourselves—with the rest of the party going on. But wait, it gets worse! When the cake came out and everyone gathered around to sing "Happy Birthday," where was Sarah?

Under the picnic table. She had her hands over her ears and was just rocking.

That was the first time my heart broke over her autism. We left right after that. It was sensory overload for her, but we didn't understand at the time that was what was happening. I remember getting in the car and just crying with my ex-husband. I'm talking SOBBBBBINGG.

We thought this would be our future, forever. Our child not able to function with other kids her age and being singled out, and us being frazzled forever running behind her to "save her."

Flash forward. There's hope with all of this. I don't want to be Debbie Downer.

Sarah has come into her own, and she'll throw up deuces to anyone who doesn't like her. But for a long time, our reality was as I described before. Sarah will be 12 this year, and this will be the first birthday that we won't do all the fanfare. She has found her tribe with two girls, and that's enough for her. It's enough for her dad and me, too.

One of the things that I wanted to do in my chapter is to make sure I help parents like myself struggling with birthday isolations. Here is my advice:

1.) First of all, I want to make sure that parents know that they're not alone. It helps to talk to other parents in your community who have kids on the spectrum. Find YOUR PARENT

Who's There When It's Time to Blow out the Candles

TRIBE because y'all are going to be together for a while.

2.) Reach out to the school counselor and your PTA/HSA, and ask them what type of education they could offer to kids and parents about autism.

3.) Get involved as much as you can at school functions. The more parents get to know you, the better it will be for your child.

4.) In terms of birthday parties, be PREPARED!

a) Figure out the roadblocks ahead of time with food choices and/or sensory overload either at their own party OR at the one they're going to attend.

b) Accept what's going to happen is what's going to happen. It will not be the end of the world.

c) Don't have any expectations of what a birthday party is "supposed to be" or how your child is "supposed to act."

d) Stay at the party your child is going to and always have an exit plan.

e) Give the hosting parents a heads up about how your child acts and what they might need.

f) Contact the venue of the birthday party (whether it's your child's birthday or the friend's) and talk to them about their ability to accommodate children on the spectrum.

You're going to get through every birthday. I promise you that. Some of them may be harder than others, but as long as you stay positive, don't expect too much, and fill them with love, you'll be "AUlright."

Who's There When It's Time to Blow out the Candles

Photographer: Heidi Iliff

Holly Teegarden is a digital marketing consultant, national speaker on social media and analytics, autism advocate, digital detox expert, certified Christian Life Coach, and doTERRA Wellness Advocate. She sounds busy (I AM). She lives in Sewickley, PA, with her husband and her daughter Sarah. Holly is active in her community as the cofounder of the Quaker Valley Special Education Parent Networking Group and with her church, North Way Christian Community Sewickley Valley. Holly has a degree in English literature from Nazareth College in Rochester, NY. She dreamed of finishing college and writing for a living. This book is the start of that dream coming true.

KJ's Autism . . . A Mother's Inspiration

Lenore Wossidlo

"It's tough living with a sibling who has autism. Sometimes you wish they didn't have autism. Sometimes you wish that you were a single child. But in the end, you always love them. No matter what they do, no matter how they act, through the toughest times, the bonds of family will keep you and your sibling with autism together."

~ Paul J. Wossidlo, Age 15 (now a college freshman)

It has been said that GOD gives you what you can handle. GOD trusted us a lot! He gave us a child with special needs whom we could take care of and prepare for a productive life.

KJ's Autism . . . A Mother's Inspiration

KJ was diagnosed with autism on September 25, 1995. I remember it well because it was Yom Kippur, the holiest day of the Jewish religion. We should have been celebrating the New Year, and this was how it started—with a diagnosis of autism.

KJ

Karl Joseph (KJ) Wossidlo was born on Monday, December 14, 1992, at 6:40 a.m. He had his days and nights mixed up for about a year. KJ had to be completely asleep before I could put him in the crib. I would walk him to sleep between 1 and 2 a.m., while watching reruns of *Maude, The Golden Girls*, and *Cheers*, as well as *The Weather Channel*.

KJ started walking at 14 months and talking at 18 months. He only said a few words, with "Mama" being the first word he said. We were not concerned yet though because I was a late talker, and I knew that every child reached milestones when they are ready.

The pediatrician asked me what words he said at 18 months; it was only five words. He asked me again at the two-year visit, and I was speechless.

KJ said no words.

Our pediatrician said that we should wait six more months, since he might be a late talker. At his 2.5 year visit, the pediatrician gave me a prescription and contact information to start testing for speech delays.

We did not know how to talk about it, what to talk about, or how to feel. We had no comparison, since KJ is our first child. However, we trusted our pediatrician to guide us, since he quickly picked up on the fact that KJ may have autism.

My husband Paul and I had suspected for some time that something was wrong. Music would soothe KJ, so we had calming cassettes and CDs in the car when we took him out. If we were indoors and he fussed, I would sing to him to calm him down. That was until he realized how bad my singing is! Then he would cover his ears because of my singing voice.

His language skills had disappeared, and he could not tell us what he wanted. He didn't point or gesture, and he cried a lot, even if I left the room for a few seconds. He was frustrated and did not nap! He would go-go-go for 15 straight hours! His record is 19 straight hours without a nap.

As time passed, we saw hand-flapping, and he covered his ears when he heard loud noises and his eyes when he saw bright neon colors, especially during cosmic bowling.

Our concerns led us to Karleen Preator at Children's Hospital CDU in Pittsburgh for a formal diagnosis. I remember driving home in tears thinking, "What next? What lies ahead for us?"

Two weeks later, Dr. Preator met with us to discuss the diagnosis and how to proceed. She also encouraged us to BELIEVE in KJ's future, which we did!

After the shock wore off and we started down the path of teaching KJ, I learned sign language to help us communicate.

PLEA—an educational and advocacy organization that helps people with disabilities function to their fullest potential in the community—felt just right for us. Just three months after he started there, he was communicating with pictures! This is how we knew that KJ was extremely visual. PLEA was his foundation for success.

KJ started attending a toddler group and then transitioned to PLEA preschool in January 1996. He needed structure, but could he handle five days a week, five hours a day? Could I? About two weeks after he started at PLEA, I got into my car after dropping him off and started bawling my eyes out. My baby's going to preschool, he has a backpack, and I packed him a lunch—major accomplishments!

Therapy cats have also been a big part of our work with KJ. Wednesday, our first therapy cat, came to us in June of 1999. My sister-in-law purchased a gift certificate for us from the Western PA Humane Society, after our very first cat, Cuddles, crossed over the rainbow bridge in November 1998.

KJ loves the cats, especially the calmer ones. He loves to pet them. We have shown him how to pick up the cats when he needs to move them. I always bring up a cat to say goodnight to KJ.

KJ and PJ

We always wanted two children, no matter their gender. We waited until KJ was in school full time to have another child.

On March 5, 2000, Paul Joseph Wossidlo (PJ) was born. One of the challenges we faced as PJ got older was giving him enough quality time without KJ. We learned this by trial-and-error, and we communicate with PJ and listen to his concerns. We work as a family team to resolve issues.

It is a daily juggling act, balancing our work schedule with KJ getting on and off the ACCESS bus. I have hand-to-hand services for him, meaning that the ACCESS driver must pick up and drop off KJ to a person, not just at the front door.

PJ is still learning about KJ's unique needs. He defends KJ and even sometimes will help ME stay calm. I remember one time when KJ was coming home and walking up the porch steps with one of his aides. PJ and I were next door, along with some other neighbors. One of the kids started laughing at KJ. PJ said, very emphatically, "Don't you laugh at him. He is my brother!"

KJ tries his best to be a "big brother" to PJ. He knows it is hard because of his autism. He has apologized to PJ many times. All he really wants is acceptance from PJ, and everyone, as to how unique he is.

KJ's Bar Mitzvah

As KJ approached 12, and I realized he would be 13 the following year, I started thinking about his Bar Mitzvah. This would be challenging. How would we do it? Who would come? With our rabbi, we discussed how important it would be to

KJ and to us as a family. It was important to us because I felt it would bring us together in a way that no other event could. I would help him prepare.

We enrolled him in a religious school for special needs. We discussed with the rabbi what was important for him to consider it complete. We laid out a plan to prepare KJ with the four items that would make it official. This included rehearsals, making a picture schedule for the congregation to see and a smaller one for KJ to use, and deciding who would be invited. This needed to be a small event. I had help from several individuals and a couple of Jewish organizations.

On Sunday, August 20, 2006, KJ celebrated his Bar Mitzvah with sign language and pictures in front of very close family and friends, many of them with autism. We had a small reception afterwards, and we breathed a sigh of relief! We were very proud of our son with autism for accomplishing this major task.

Community and Law Enforcement

When I realized how strong KJ was at age 5, I thought to myself, what if he hit a police officer? Would they understand? In 1998, my ongoing project began to help law enforcement understand the characteristics of autism, tips on how to recognize it, and suggested ways to handle situations.

This was so well received in the law enforcement community! Police officers, fire departments, and emergency service personnel want to know this information. I spoke to my local police department in Swissvale. This led to a television appearance and newspaper articles, as well as many presentations.

Making your local first responders aware of your child with special needs will help immensely, if any emergency were to occur. Think about how emergency personnel would respond to certain things your child does? How would your child respond in an emergency? What do you need to do or to tell a first responder to have a more positive outcome?

With the help of several police departments and the Woodland Hills Theater Department, I produced a video illustrating different scenarios, details about the scenarios, and suggested ways to handle them. The police departments also helped me make copies for Allegheny County police departments and the PA State Chiefs of Police Convention in Lancaster, PA.

It is critical to have an information form on file with your local police department, as well as police departments in the areas that you vacation in, and a brief form in the glove compartment. I say brief because they need the info as quickly as they can get it. Make sure you tell the dispatcher that there is someone with autism involved in the situation you are calling about. Check with your local police department or online for police forms for individuals with special needs.

It is sometimes necessary to have stickers and/or magnets on your car windows and bumpers that say, "Child with autism; may not respond to verbal commands." You can add "non-verbal." This will help them be more prepared and think outside the box.

Today

On May 29, 2014, KJ accomplished a major goal: he walked across the stage with his diploma from Spectrum Charter School. Spectrum Charter School looked for the skills KJ had and helped him excel so that he could find work he enjoyed. He was even able to volunteer with Westmoreland County Food Bank thanks to the skills he developed at school. He still holds the record of folding 170 boxes in 2 hours there. In May of 2008, KJ was named Volunteer of the

Month for his packing, stacking, and moving boxes of food in a timely manner.

He now works full time at Milestones Prevocational Center in Monroeville, PA and loves working! He is still getting used to shorter holiday breaks and working in the summer. We are also realizing that just like everyone else, he needs holiday breaks and a vacation. KJ also enjoys playing Miracle League baseball. I believe he loves it because he has played baseball on the Wii for many years.

Today, KJ knows more sign language than I do. I have also taught him some of the Jewish prayers in sign language, which we now sign at the Mostly Musical Shabbat services on the first Friday of each month. KJ hears and understands everything we say (sometimes too much). He needs help to answer us and to express his feelings.

KJ's autism is truly a mother's ... *my* ... inspiration.

When I am having a bad day, KJ comes over to me and hugs and kisses me. Even if his behavior is the reason for the day not going so well, how can I refuse that?

When life's challenges have taken over, I ask GOD to show me the way. And if it is not the time, I ask him to show me a sign that it all will work out, just to keep me feeling positive. HE does show me the way!

Why is this important? Because you will have so many more challenges and questions along the way. You will cry, scream, wonder, laugh, smile. ASK FOR HELP; IT'S OKAY! It is a sign that you need help and you recognize it's time to ask!

Looking ahead and planning for future services should always be on your radar. What is the next step for your child? Always think, what if? What is the best situation for MY child? How will MY child learn best and how do we make that happen?

In many situations, kids with autism cannot generalize. They think, "I do this only at school. I do this only with staff." If services are not working for you, think outside the box, and speak up! Find out why they are not working and what can be changed to make it work. Sometimes the change can be something as little as how your words are phrased. This is your child, and you are their advocate!

KJ's Autism . . . A Mother's Inspiration

Photographer:

Paul Richard Wossidlo Photography

Lenore Wossidlo lives in Pittsburgh, PA, with her husband Paul, her sons Karl Joseph (KJ) and Paul Joseph (PJ), and her cats. She has been an advocate for autism for many years, marching on the steps of the Capitol Building in Harrisburg when Pennsylvania wanted to make changes to the Medical Assistance program and cut services. She has participated in walk-a-thons for autism and has spoken to many departments and associations about autism for emergency responders. She promotes awareness about autism's characteristics and offers suggestions to produce a positive outcome. Her inspiration for writing comes from her late grandfather, Dr. Joseph H. Greenberg. Her determination and persistence in life comes from her late mother, Sylvia G.

Sadwick. She published her book KJ's Autism: A Mother's Inspiration in 2015.

Resources

Discovering the Diagnosis, and What to Do Next (In No Particular Order)

By Catherine A. Hughes

"Autism can't define me. I define autism."

~ Kerry Magro

"Cathy ..." he said gently. "No, this is not your fault. It's nobody's fault. But PDD-NOS . . . it is on what we call 'the spectrum.' Cathy, your son has a form of autism."

As I described in my chapter, I felt everything around me disappear when Dr. Newman provided me with the answer to what seemed like a million questions about my then three-year-old son's mannerisms, behaviors, and skill deficits. I was sad. I was angry. I was relieved. I was scared. I was confused. I was worried. I was all of these emotions with a side of about seventeen more.

Ok, maybe more like 286.

However, I learned what my son was experiencing, and that there was a lot to be done. And I do mean, *a lot*.

Everyone absorbs their loved one's diagnosis in different ways. There is not a right or wrong way to process what you have been told, how to grieve what you feel as if you may have lost, and there are certainly no timeframes. In fact, being perfectly truthful, I often move through feelings of grief and frustration nearing two decades later as I delicately (sometimes, as delicate as a manic bull in a china shop) perform the dance between light support as to be respectful of his choices as a self-advocate and smothering him to ensure he has what he needs to live an abundant life.

Though some roads will intersect with others along the way, ultimately everyone's roadmap is different. That being said, I believe that anyone can find value in taking the following steps on their path:

1.) Preserve yourself by means of proper self-care so you can be at your best. Being at your best is not just so you can support your child and is not just to be present for your entire family who is also experiencing a multitude of emotions. Being at your best is what you deserve. The cartoon of the mother who puts the oxygen mask on herself prior to her child on the turbulent airplane was created to prove a valid point. Self-care is far from selfish, and this phrase is far from cliché. Set yourself up for success by valuing your own needs.

2.) You need to allow yourself to move through your feelings. The mad feelings. The sad feelings. The roller coaster feelings. The paralyzed and can't move a muscle feelings. The "I have no idea what ABA-IEP-SLP-AAC stands for" feelings. The "Will she ever make a friend?" feelings. The "When will he tell me about his school day?" feelings. The "I'm sick of all these appointments!" feelings. The powerless feelings. The superhero complex feelings. Your feelings exist, they are valid, and they need felt. They aren't wrong.

3.) Let's talk about those feelings for a moment. Stop blaming yourself. You. Right now. Never again. This diagnosis is not anyone's fault. Autism is a lifelong neurological difference, and some would say that the disability experience is simply a different way of being.

Others would confirm that the challenges that accompany this diagnosis can be downright exhausting, devastating, and heart-wrenching. Everyone's experience differs, but one commonality amongst everyone is that no one is to blame.

4.) Yes indeed, it's time to "get to gettin'." It's homework time! It's time to learn about what autism is, and what it isn't. The information about the diagnosis itself, community supports and clinical services that you'll find across the internet and within literature (oh you know, like a book written by a group of moms) overflows compared to the turn of the century. Of course, along the way, you will encounter Negative Nancies (if your name is "Nancy," I apologize), come across snake oils, and perhaps become enticed by magical potions that claim that they can make your loved one's autism disappear. Notice I said "claim," and by "claim," I'm trying to tell you to run for the hills.

5.) Secure quality services from qualified professionals, and obtain an Individualized Education Plan (IEP) within the school system. Often, a child with autism is enrolled in Early Intervention (depending on the age of diagnosis), a program grounded in Applied Behavior Analysis (ABA), occupational therapy, and speech therapy. Other supports could include physical therapy (for children with hypotonia, or low muscle tone), music therapy, play therapy, or social skills groups (to name just a few). If your region has case managers or care coordinators available to assist in moving through red tape, by all means, open a case. Also be sure that your medical team, especially the psychologist or developmental pediatrician, provides you ample time during appointments to answer all of your questions and point you in the right direction. The more allies on your side, the easier it is to advocate for what is needed for both your child and the entire family unit.

6.) Seek out grants, funding, and community outreach in your area. Though more sparse than we would like, there are programs that exist to fund items from iPads and adaptive bicycles to summer camps to fences and alarms for your home. It doesn't hurt to find out if your church provides meals to struggling families or search for a parent group that will trade off respite days. Just ASK. And don't give up.

7.) Nurture all of your relationships. In addition to not neglecting yourself, do not ignore your spouse, siblings, extended family members, or friends by getting wrapped up in "autism superhero" mode. Help extended family members (grandparents, aunts, uncles, cousins) understand what you are experiencing and learn how to help you and your family. Nine times out of ten, people want to be supportive rather than turn the other cheek. They just don't know what they don't know.

8.) Become a Sherlock Holmes and investigate any other medical conditions or nutritional deficiencies that could be underlying that your child cannot find the right words to express (gut issues, sleeping, pain, malabsorption, etc.). It is not uncommon for someone with autism to experience either heightened pain, or not recognize how ill they may be due to desensitization as a result of sensory dysfunction. It's no wonder, then why sometimes maladaptive behaviors manifest as a result. No one functions well when they feel sick. We often hurt, and we experience brain fog, don't we? Imagine what someone with autism might feel like, given their struggles.

9.) Please, listen to autistic adults, or as they call proudly themselves: #ActuallyAutistic. It is very easy to get caught up in the idea that we have to "fix" every "behavior" that appears "wrong." Ethical, clinically sound and respectful ABA and Positive Behavior Support approaches tell us that we need to address the antecedents and consequences of behaviors that interfere with daily functioning, social interaction with peers, and ultimate independence. Remember, behaviors are any means of how one conducts themselves, and behaviors do not equal tantrums. For that matter, no two "tantrums" look alike between two children. A friend of mine—a proud autistic self-advocate—urges today's society to challenge everything we think we know. Let's consider that someone with autism is not functioning inherently wrong, just because our non-autistic perspective would lead us to believe so. Every behavior serves a purpose, which is what ABA allows us to examine. Together with our diagnosed loved ones at the table, no matter where on the spectrum they fall, we can craft a plan for success and be a part of the same world.

10.) I had to save the best for last—FIND YOUR TRIBE! I have never met a parent or caregiver who said that their strongest advice didn't come from someone raising someone with autism. We laugh together when the sensory bin of beans spills across the floor. We cry on each other's shoulders when talking about our mutual lack of sleep because our kids suffer from insomnia and get up at 4 am to bang pots in the kitchen to make music. We learn from each other when we share information about the amazing speech therapist that is 40 minutes away from home but is making leaps and bounds with the children they are treating. Find support groups in your area. Find Facebook groups to connect with other families at any time of the day, from anywhere, and while wearing your pajamas. Use apps that link you to others JUST. LIKE. YOU. I assure you, I promise you, with every cell in my body, you are not and never will be alone. If you truly feel as if you are, I am happy to tell you that our tribe is always accepting new members.

May I take your hand?

Finding Your Tribe: Forming a Parent Networking Group

By Holly Teegarden

One of the things I have realized over the years is the importance of having a "tribe" when it comes to having a child on the spectrum, which is why I loved being part of this book!

I started a special education parent-networking group in my school district after realizing something was missing with the PTA/HSA groups. It has been a godsend for a lot of parents who need to bounce ideas off of fellow parents, schedule play dates or learn from our monthly speakers. The group is comprised of parents whose children have IEPs, 504 plans, speech services, and/or reading challenges. The overall goal is to provide a place for parents to network with other parents "like them" and to get educated by relevant presenters. Another goal is to work alongside the school district to make the special education program even better for our children. In two years, we've grown our district's group to around 100 people and continue to expand it.

So, how did we get the ball rolling?

I knew two other moms that felt frustrated and alone. They too were trying to navigate the special education seas in our district. I thought if these two moms and I were dealing with this, others must be too. We met and realized that we could change our community. It was then that we decided to form a group.

Here's how to do just that:

1.) **Create a private online space for your group.** For us, that was important for people to feel as if they could speak freely about what was happening in their schools. We decided to use a private Facebook group with prerequisite questions that we asked parents to screen them. I would highly suggest going this route. The group can still be searchable online, but no one but the members can see its content. The three of us had friends, and we invited those friends who invited *their* friends and so on. My group has parents and caregivers from two elementary schools, one middle school, and the high school.

2.) **Get the word out.** We created flyers and placed them around the community and schools and in school publications. We even reached out to the local newspaper to run a story about what we were doing.

3.) **Divide and conquer.** Figure out who does what with the group if you start it with other people. You might have someone who has connections and can reach out to potential speakers, someone who knows marketing, someone who loves the hospitality piece of the meetings, etc. It's essential to set roles so efforts are not duplicated.

4.) **Create a survey.** We use Google Forms for our surveys. We do an anonymous "customer satisfaction" form for our school district at the beginning and end of the school year to gauge how people feel about what's happening. The three founders of the group meet with the superintendent of our school district to review the findings, and then we let the group know the results as well. We have also distributed surveys to understand what people want out of the group. Surveys are a great way to gain clarity about people's needs.

5.) **Connect with the school district.** This might take baby steps, depending on how open the parents are within your school(s). It is vital that you try to align with them as the leader of your group. We have had our superintendent as one of the monthly speakers, and next school year we're growing that presence by welcoming other members of the district. The goal should be working with them, not against them.

6.) **Meet with the PTA/HSA leaders.** These parents represent the greater good for each school. Meeting with them allowed our group to explain what we were trying to create, get insight on speakers, and build a bridge of positive communication.

7.) **Find a physical place to meet.** One of the questions that we asked in our survey is when people could meet and how often. We were trying to figure out if we could gather at a coffee house, library, etc. We were able to secure a location for our meetings—for free!— at a local learning center. We realized early on that we wanted a space that was private so no one could "listen in" on our conversations. Creating a safe environment for your members is so important.

8.) **Find speakers.** Most people will speak for free to your group. Every month, we have special education lawyers, advocates, speech pathologists, etc. who speak for us. What's great is that, each time, you can walk away with something new! Based on who comprises your group, you'll be able to better determine what type of speakers you want for your meetings.

9.) **Publicize your speakers.** Because we're not a sanctioned group with the school district, any publicity for our group is on us. For our monthly speakers, we reach out to our local newspaper, we ask that events be listed on the school district calendar and in school newsletters, and then obviously, we promote them on social media where so many of our members are.

10.) **Let conversations happen in the group.** In our group, we do not try to push the conversation. I think it's important that people build relationships and connect organically.

There is so much value in having a tribe within your school district that you can go to for questions when it comes to special education. We have been able to help parents with IEPs, teacher challenges, finding friends, and a wealth of other things. It takes some legwork, but with a little help, you can build a community that

Finding Your Tribe

creates lasting change where you live and where your child goes to school.

Top 5 Tips for a Successful IEP Meeting

By Christina Abernethy

1.) Make a list.

Sometime before your meeting, make a list of things you want to discuss during an individualized education plan (IEP) meeting. These can include anything new going on, current behavior concerns, academics, therapies, etc. I write mine down in bullet points so it's easy to read and I can cross off items as they are addressed. Include any questions you might have prior to the meeting to make sure they are answered before the meeting is over.

2.) Bring someone with you.

Many people are unaware that you can bring someone with you to your meeting! This person can be your spouse, a caregiver, a friend, another family member, a service coordinator, or anyone else that you feel would help advocate for what's best for your child. It is your right, and you are permitted to bring anyone you'd like with you. If you do not have anyone to ask or to bring with you, reach out to your child's school. They should be able to provide you with someone to help support you and your family during the meeting.

3.) Make it personal.

You know your child BEST! Bring something with you that allows everyone to see your child the way you do. So how do you do that? You can bring a photo of your child or make an "All About Me" page or Vision Statement as described in this book (visit that section to learn how to create them). Things to think about before creating these documents are your child's strengths, goals, reinforcers, and more. Once you have made your page(s) and printed it out, put it in a plastic cover for protection. You can pass this around at the meeting or you can print one for each teacher and/or therapist who will be working with your child. The purpose of "making it personal" is for everyone to get to know your child better. They need to know what they can do to help your child learn and grow. Every single person working with your child has an important role in their life. It is up to us to give them the tools they need to help them achieve their goals, become the best they can be, and ultimately find their voice.

4.) Take notes during the meeting.

Often during IEP meetings, A LOT of information is discussed. It can be overwhelming sometimes and may be too much to remember. Someone might use an acronym you never heard of before or recommend a new therapy, and you don't want to forget to look it up when you get home. If you have something with you to take notes, you can write a few things down that you can address at the end of the meeting. You can also use the notes as reference or reminders of things to do next or things your child is currently working on. If you have a folder that you keep with important information about your child, you can put this in there as well.

5.) Do not sign anything that makes you uncomfortable or that you do not agree with.

You do not have to sign anything that you are unsure about or do not agree with in part or full. It is your right to ask for a copy, take it home, review it, and then decide if everything is the way you want or need it to be. It is a good idea to review the documents with your spouse, a doctor, a friend, or anyone you trust. You can also ask for another meeting to discuss and clarify things you are concerned about or elements of it that you do not understand. Service coordinators or a local advocate can be a huge help in reviewing paperwork. Once you are happy with the documents and everything is as it should be, *then* you should sign it.

I would also like to add that if your child is older and able to be present during the meeting prior to transition, please bring them with you. If they are able to communicate their wants and needs or likes and dislikes, let them participate! As parents and caregivers, we are here to help guide them and advocate for them when they are not able to. But what is even more important and amazing to watch is when they can advocate for themselves and use their own voices in a powerful and meaningful way.

Last, but not least, end on a positive note. IEP meetings can be stressful and overwhelming. Talking about things that your child can't do or all of the extra support needed can make you feel sad or upset. I think it's important for us to end a meeting talking about our child's strengths, what they CAN do, and how we move forward from that point!

To watch a video summary of these tips, you can go to http://bit.ly/IEPMeetingSuccess.

All About Me Pages and Vision Statements

By Christina Abernethy

All About Me pages and Vision Statements are a great resource to provide during meetings or for any person who will be working with your child. The pages offer a personal touch, enabling people to see your child for who they truly are and to focus on the child's strengths to ultimately guide them to become the best that they can be.

Many different tools can be used for creating an All About Me page or a Vision Statement document. Two of my favorites are the Canva app or Microsoft Word. The Canva app is free and can be downloaded onto your computer, laptop, or phone.

All About Me Pages

Before you start creating an All About Me page, you may want to make a list or outline. I have created a list of suggestions to guide you in creating a personalized page for your child. The examples are there to give you ideas, but use what is best to describe your child and their needs. There are no right or wrong categories!

- Name (you can add a nickname too, if they have one)

- Grade

- Picture of your child

- Things that motivate your child

  ➢ Praise, rewards, food, toys, iPad time/videos, outdoor play

- What works well for your child

  ➢ Routine, picture cards, patience, social stories, positive reinforcement

- What does not work well for your child

  ➢ Negative talk, yelling, being rushed, loud noises

- What are your child's strengths

  ➢ Good listener, works well with others, happy, fluent reader

- What are your child's goals for this year

  ➢ Reading, writing, cutting with scissors independently, conversational speech, life skills

Vision Statements

When creating a Vision Statement for your child, add a photo or two to make it personal, just like the All About Me page. Evaluate what they love and capitalize on their strengths. What do you want for your child as they get older? What could you envision them doing for a job? How do you envision them as an adult living a happy and successful life?

A Vision Statement can be as long or short as you would like it to be. A shorter vision statement could be added to your All About Me page. You can also create a longer Vision Statement and have it on a separate page by itself.

Please note, "All About Me" pages and Vision Statements will change every year. As your child gets older, the goal is for them to create their own documents or help create a new one. This will allow them to use their own voice and communicate what they want for themselves and their future. This is true person-centered planning.

Author's Blogs or Websites

Autism Caring Center:
https://autismcaringcenter.com

Changing Spaces Pennsylvania
https://www.facebook.com/groups/ChangingSp
acesPA/

Discovery Toys (Consultant - Lenore Wossidlo)
http://www.lenztoyz.com

Everyday Life Coach:
http://bit.ly/EverydayLifeCoach

Labeled to Lunderful:
http://www.labeledtolunderful.com

Living in Boldness:
http://livinginboldness.com

Love, Hope & Autism
https://lovehopeandautism.com

All About Me Pages and Vision Statements

Our Trolley Ride with Autism
https://www.facebook.com/ourtrolleyridewithautism/

Team Cassie Fund
https://pittsburghfoundation.org/team-cassie

The Caffeinated Advocate
http://caffeinatedadvocate.wordpress.com

Some of Our Favorite Websites

Achieving True Self

www.achievingtrueself.com

Advancing Futures for Adults with Autism:

www.afaa-us.org

Agile Instruction and Management Solutions (AIMS)

www.aimsinstruction.com

American Academy of Child & Adolescent Psychiatry

www.aacap.org/aacap/families_and_youth/reso urce_centers/Autism_Resource_Center/Home.a spx

You are Not Alone

American Occupational Therapy Association
www.aota.org/About-Occupational-Therapy/PatientsClients/ChildrenAndYouth

American Speech-Language-Hearing Association
www.asha.org/public/speech/disorders/Autism
www.asha.org/Practice-Portal/Clinical-Topics/Autism

The ARC (There are chapters around the country.)
www.thearc.org

ASERT
www.paautism.org

Autism Asperger's Digest
www.autismdigest.com

Autism Connection of PA
www.autismofpa.org

Autism Navigator®
http://autismnavigator.com

Autism NOW
https://autismnow.org/

Autism Society of America
http://www.autism-society.org/what-is/

Autism Speaks
www.autismspeaks.org

The Autistic Self-Advocacy Network
www.autisticadvocacy.org

The Autistic Women and Nonbinary Network
www.awnnetwork.org

Behavior Analyst Certification Board
https://www.bacb.com

The Center for Autism
www.thecenterforautism.org

Future Horizons
https://www.fhautism.com/

You are Not Alone

Jeannette Purkiss | Autistic Advocate, Author, and Speaker

http://www.jeanettepurkis.com/

MAX-Ability

http://max-ability.com

National Autism Association

http://nationalautismassociation.org/

PEAL Center (Parent Education & Advocacy Leadership)

www.pealcenter.org

Signing Time Videos

https://www.signingtime.com/

SPARK

www.sparkforautism.org

TFH USA

https://www.specialneedstoys.com/usa

The Autism Community in Action

https://tacanow.org/

Twainbow

https://www.twainbow.org

Understanding Autism, The Basics | WebMD

ttps://www.webmd.com/brain/autism/understa
nding-autism-basics#1

Wolf + Friends

https://www.wolfandfriends.com/

WrightsLaw

www.wrightslaw.com

Some "Ausome" Apps We Wanted to Share

ABA Flash Cards and Games: Emotions—App Store

Autism Therapy with MITA—Amazon Fire, App Store, GooglePlay

Autism Parenting Magazine—App Store, GooglePlay

Daycape—App Store, GooglePlay

Endless Alphabet—App Store, GooglePlay

Find a Friend—App Store, GooglePlay

Mood Meter—App Store, GooglePlay

Proloquo2Go—App Store

Screen Time for Kids—Amazon Fire, App Store, GooglePlay

Sesame Street and Autism—App Store, GooglePlay

Wolf + Friends—App Store, GooglePlay

Our Favorite Websites